Routledge Revivals

The Development of Sacramentalism

First published in 1928, *The Development of Sacramentalism* traces the history of the fundamental presuppositions upon which the doctrine of sacraments is built from primitive religions, through the Old Testament and the Mystery Cults. This book will be of interest to students of history and religion.

The Development of Sacramentalism

J. W. C. Wand

First published in 1928
By Methuen & Co. Ltd.

This edition first published in 2024 by Routledge
4 Park Square, Milton Park, Abingdon, Oxon, OX14 4RN
and by Routledge
605 Third Avenue, New York, NY 10017

Routledge is an imprint of the Taylor & Francis Group, an informa business

© J. W. C. Wand 1928

All rights reserved. No part of this book may be reprinted or reproduced or utilised in any form or by any electronic, mechanical, or other means, now known or hereafter invented, including photocopying and recording, or in any information storage or retrieval system, without permission in writing from the publishers.

Publisher's Note
The publisher has gone to great lengths to ensure the quality of this reprint but points out that some imperfections in the original copies may be apparent.

Disclaimer
The publisher has made every effort to trace copyright holders and welcomes correspondence from those they have been unable to contact.

ISBN: 978-1-032-73504-7 (hbk)
ISBN: 978-1-003-46451-8 (ebk)
ISBN: 978-1-032-73505-4 (pbk)

Book DOI 10.4324/9781003464518

THE DEVELOPMENT OF SACRAMENTALISM

BY

J. W. C. WAND, M.A.
FELLOW, DEAN AND TUTOR OF ORIEL COLLEGE, OXFORD
EXAMINING CHAPLAIN TO THE BISHOP OF PETERBOROUGH

METHUEN & CO. LTD.
36 ESSEX STREET W.C.
LONDON

First Published in 1928

PRINTED IN GREAT BRITAIN

UXORI DILECTISSIMAE
STUDIORUM OXONIENSIUM
PRIMITIAS

PREFACE

A WORD or two must be said in order to explain the purpose of this book. It does not set out to discuss the doctrine of the sacraments, but to trace the history of the fundamental presupposition upon which that doctrine is built. Perhaps this will become clearer if we trace the meaning of the terms employed.

The word 'sacrament' has a long history behind it, to the course of which three main sources have contributed. It is derived from the Latin *sacrare*, 'to dedicate,' and was used as a technical military term for the oath by which a soldier pledged his allegiance to his commander or to the emperor himself. But its form is passive, and in that sense it was used for the sum of money deposited by the parties to a lawsuit as a pledge of good faith. Thirdly, it was employed to translate the Greek word for 'mystery,' which itself had had a complicated history, and was in fact used to denote both a secret rite and a revealed truth.

It is obvious that in these circumstances the word has been, and still is, capable of a very varied significance. It may be narrowed down to mean nothing but the Christian Eucharist, or it may be widened out to cover almost any statement that implies religious verity. And even among those who use it solely for certain rites and ceremonies it still conceals a curious ambiguity, for to one it may mean only a pictorial representation of spiritual truth, while to another it can only imply the conveyance of spiritual grace through specific material means.

It is for this reason that I prefer the word 'sacramentalism' as the title of our theme. For sacramentalism may be taken to mean the habit of thought and practice that sees physical things and uses them as the vehicles of spiritual power. The fact that the word is generally employed by opponents, and has about it a certain invidious flavour, makes its meaning all the clearer. I accept it in its sharpest sense, and proceed to consider the forms under which the principle has manifested and sought to explain itself from the earliest times to the present day.

Small as this book is, I find it impossible to mention the names of all the scholars whose knowledge of special periods has helped in the preparation of it. One who has but recently taken up residence in Oxford finds an unfailing source of gratitude in the fact that so many veterans on the field of learning are ready to share their spoils with a new-comer. But I must at least offer my thanks to Dr. Darwell Stone, who read the work in manuscript and made some valuable suggestions, and to Professor D. C. Simpson, without whose friendly criticism and continual encouragement the book would never have seen the light. I am also much indebted to my pupil, the Reverend H. Thomas, who prepared the index. For such views here advanced as may ultimately prove erroneous, I have no one to thank but myself.

J. W. C. WAND

ORIEL COLLEGE, OXFORD
20th August 1928

CONTENTS

CHAP.		PAGE
I. Primitive Ideas and Customs		1
II. Old Testament		15
III. Sacrifice as Sacrament		31
IV. The Hebrew Prophets		44
V. The Mystery Religions		58
VI. The Background of Christianity		68
VII. Teaching of Jesus		82
VIII. The Apostolic Church		94
IX. The Ante-Nicene Fathers		110
X. The Middle Ages		124
XI. The Reformation and After		141
XII. Modern Views and Difficulties		153
Selected Book List		167
Index		171

THE DEVELOPMENT OF SACRAMENTALISM

CHAPTER I

PRIMITIVE IDEAS AND CUSTOMS

WHEN the Spaniards first penetrated into Peru they were much interested in the religious customs of the people of that land. In particular they observed that at the great feast of Raymi there was placed upon the royal board a cake of fine bread, prepared by the Virgins of the Sun, together with goblets of the fermented liquor of the country. These the Inca himself first tasted and then passed round among the assembled nobles. 'In the distribution of bread and wine at this high festival,' says Prescott,[1] 'the orthodox Spaniards saw a striking resemblance to the Christian communion; as in the practice of confession and penance, which, in a most irregular form indeed, seems to have been used by the Peruvians, they discerned a coincidence with another of the sacraments of the Church. The good fathers were fond of tracing such coincidences, which they considered as the contrivance of Satan,

[1] *Conquest of Peru* (1847), i. 102.

who thus endeavoured to delude his victims by counterfeiting the blessed rites of Christianity.'

Such was the opinion of the orthodox in the sixteenth century : Pagan rites were the satanic counterfeits of Christian sacraments. But the opinion is older than that. It is found already in Tertullian, who at the end of the second century complains that 'the Devil . . . rivals the very realities of the Divine sacraments in the idol-mysteries.'[1] Further back, in the middle of the second century, Justin Martyr had explained that the use of bread and a cup of water by those who were to be initiated into the mysteries of Mithras was due to the imitation of Christianity by the 'evil demons.'[2] And it is possible that the source of this view may be found in S. Paul's own comparison of the table of the Lord with the table of devils.[3] However, a great change has come over our ways of thinking since then. That there was borrowing is quite possible, though many modern scholars would say that it is the Christians who have borrowed from the Pagans. An attempt to adjudicate between these rival theories will be made later. But for the present we must remind ourselves that we no longer have any need to postulate diabolical agency in order to explain these parallels between Pagan and Christian rites. The comparative study of religion has made it clear that both alike rest upon a foundation that is to be found in all religion as far back as history and anthropology will take us. That foundation is the sacramental principle, the belief in the transmission of spiritual power by

[1] *Praesc. Her.* xl.   [2] *Apol.* lxvi. 4.   [3] 1 Cor. x. 21.

PRIMITIVE IDEAS AND CUSTOMS

material means. Our first task must be to trace the source of this principle in the first springs of man's religious thought.

In what form religious ideas were first conceived by members of the human race is still a matter of conjecture. One theory of the anthropologists derives all from the imitative dancing with which primitive men, like children, beguiled the hours when they were not actually hunting or fighting. Soon it began to be felt that these ceremonies were acts of power, that they gave rise to an unseen influence which was potent for good or evil. Presently this power was thought to have an independent existence, it was personified under various forms, and so there came the resultant belief in spiritual existences.

By way of extreme opposition to this, Rudolph Otto, in his *Idea of the Holy*, has argued persuasively that the sense of the unseen came first in order of time, and expressed itself in the instinctive awe of the *mysterium tremendum* which is to be found not only in men, however primitive, but even in animals. In that case the rites of which we have spoken will have come in later as a means of propitiating, controlling, or otherwise influencing the unseen power.

But the point for us to notice is that whatever be the true explanation of the emergence of religious ideas, when belief in a spiritual influence does appear, that influence is never felt to be far removed from the sphere of the physical. Vast reserves of power in the unseen world were held to be accessible to primitive man through and by means of things with which he was perfectly familiar. It is this view of nature that we should call broadly sacramental. To primitive man, as to the modern poet, 'Earth's crammed with Heaven and every common bush afire with God.' 'Sacrament is rooted in nature,' says Dr. Nairne,[1] and he goes on to describe sacrament as 'natural, simple, vague, grand.' But just as life is simple and yet has many forms of self-expression, so the simplicity of sacrament resolves itself into different forms of operation. It is possible to distinguish three distinct modes in which the spiritual may be connected with the material. It can be held to reside within a material object, it can be controlled by action, it can be conveyed in a word. The vitality that gives grace to the growing tree is held to be due to this 'mana' or unseen power, which is later thought of as the spirit that resides within the circle of the spreading branches or within the narrower confines of the trunk, and has its counterpart in numberless spirits of well and river, hill and rock. Instances of the conveyance of spiritual power through action can be found not only in those imitative dances to which reference has already been made, but in many other symbolic rites that were held to ensure fertility in crops and animals or to guarantee safe deliverance in child-birth, and indeed in the whole range of what has been called 'sympathetic magic.' As for the control of supernatural power by a word, it is well known what influence primitive people still attribute to a blessing or a curse. It is seen also in the belief that a person's name may enshrine his individuality in so real a way that it may

[1] *Modern Churchman* (October 1926), pp. 304, 307.

PRIMITIVE IDEAS AND CUSTOMS 5

be used to his hurt, a belief that makes many primitive Africans of to-day as unwilling to tell a stranger their name as was the angel in the story of his wrestling with Jacob.[1] Words, in short, are as essentially capable of sacramental use as objects or actions.

It was natural that man should have recourse to this power, whether vaguely conceived or thought to proceed from definite gods or spirits, on all occasions of particular solemnity in his private or public life. The ceremonies that arose from this clearly marked tendency fall naturally into two groups—those of initiation and of the community life. It will be worth while enumerating some of the rites in either group in order that we may realize how deeply the sacramental principle entered into the very core of early religion.

I

Initiation occurred at different stages in the life of primitive man. It began at birth, when the child was received into the community. It was renewed some years later as a recognition of his arrival at the age of puberty. It might be repeated again upon his admission into some social or religious club, and it would culminate upon his accession to some position of authority. Entry upon a covenant relationship or the married state would also be regarded as needing its own rite of initiation.

At each stage it would be natural that ideas of

[1] Gen. xxxii. 29; cf. Judg. xiii. 18.

purification should dictate some elements of the ceremonies. It was equally natural for those elements to consist of bathing, washing, and other acts of cleansing. But we must not suppose that when primitive man performed these ritual acts he had in his mind modern notions of hygiene. His thought was concentrated upon their spiritual effect. His intention was not to wash away physical defilement but to remove a taboo and to get rid of any spirits that might do harm. An intensely sacramental significance was given to baptism as practised among the Egyptians at Heliopolis about the end of the fifth millennium B.C. The sun-god, Re'-Atum, was believed to be purified daily at dawn before he appeared above the horizon, either in some mythological pool, or in a sacred pool connected with his cult at Heliopolis. The king was the high priest of the god, and as such entered the temple daily at dawn in order to minister to him. But before he could minister he must himself undergo lustration. This daily baptism was explained as mediating a new birth. Just as the sun-god was himself supposed to be born daily from the water in which he was purified, so the daily lustration was supposed to bring birth to the king as son of the god. Indeed, there is evidence of baby princelings being baptized in order that they might be born again as sons of the god.[1]

An even more interesting example of the way in which a ceremony of initiation reveals this habit of

[1] See Dr. Blackman's article, 'Worship (Egyptian),' in E.R.E.

linking the spiritual with the material is to be found in the peculiar type of blood-covenant which is said to persist still in some of the Greek islands. Two youths wishing to swear eternal fidelity to each other will open a small vein in the arm and allow their blood to mingle. Thus their lives become indissolubly united; almost, it might be said, the two personalities melt into each other with the blood and become one, each of the youths regarding his friend henceforth as the other half of himself.

The use of imitative action is common in the rites that initiate couples into the estate of matrimony. A double example may be seen in the Indian custom of parting a bride's hair with a thorn. This is an imitation of the action of ploughing, and ploughing and sowing are very common adjuncts of marriage ceremonies. Their purpose is to ensure that the union shall be blest with offspring, Nature's power of fertility being regarded as one in all its manifestations.

The sacramental use of words in ceremonies of initiation is less picturesque but scarcely less important. The word sacrament itself was used of the oath taken by the Roman soldier upon his initiation into military service, and this is paralleled by the oath often taken by those who were becoming members of some more or less secret society. But a more definitely sacramental use of words will be found in those formulae of incantation which were taught to the initiates and were expected to chain the unseen powers to their will.

SACRAMENTALISM

2

The full flood of primitive sacramentalism does not burst upon us until we open up the subject of rites of the common life. Here we find that the whole structure of some societies rests upon the basis of a belief that the entire clan, and each individual member of it, shares in one life with its god. This life can be strengthened and renewed for its human partners by various means, but especially by participating in certain food and drink. It has been suggested that this belief may have been ultimately derived from the observation of the naturally stimulating effect of such refreshment upon tired and hungry people. But, however that may be, it is certain that almost from the dawn of religion one finds this belief, that by eating and drinking, communion might be made in the vital energy of the common life.

The most vivid manifestation of the idea is to be found in totemistic systems, where it is held that there exists some kind of kinship between the god, the clan, and some species of animal. This last would, of course, be held sacred, and would ordinarily be taboo. But on special occasions it would be slain, part of it given to the god and part eaten by the worshippers. So all alike would share in the common life. So strong was this feeling of a common life behind all individual existences that among some tribes even deceased members must be devoured by the surviving members in order that no part of the common stock might be lost. This was certainly

PRIMITIVE IDEAS AND CUSTOMS

the origin, and, in a sense, even the justification, of a good deal of cannibalism. A somewhat similar object of such eating was that the virtues of the deceased, whether animal or man, such as the courage of a lion or the skill of an archer, might be imbibed by the living.

This conception has been held by Dr. Robertson Smith [1] to have played a leading part in the development of sacrifice. According to his view the important element in that institution, among primitive peoples at least, was not the slaying of the victim, but the banquet, of which the slaying was a necessary preliminary. Among the tribes of South Arabia who formed the subject of his special researches it is evident that what satisfied their religious instinct was not the fact that they had offered something to God, but that in the sacrificial feast they had been able to feed upon His vital power and energy to an extent that would have been impossible by any other means.

More recently it has been suggested that there was an earlier stage in the development of sacrifice, and that at this earlier stage the rationale of the offering was to be found, not in the reception of power by the worshipper, but in the communication of vitality to the god by means of the victim that was given him. It was only in virtue of the strength so supplied that the god could perform his functions of producing heat, light, or rain for the earth. 'Originally,' says Dr. James, 'sacrifice was the food of the gods to augment their power and life, the

[1] *Religion of the Semites*, passim.

sacramental aspect growing up later as a result of the worshippers eating the remains of an offering after the blood had been poured out for the nourishment of the divinity.'[1] The only comment we need make on this is a caution against excluding a sacramental significance simply on the ground that the action is directed towards the Deity. Sacramental action may be directed up as well as down, and if primitive man identified the life with the blood his point of view was already sacramental, whether through the material substance he gave life and power to his god or received it himself.

As a god is more powerful than any animal or man, it might be presumed that a direct eating of the god himself would have corresponding advantages over the method of employing the intervention of a totemistic animal. This conclusion was actually reached by many who did in fact seek by such means to enter into immediate communion with their deities. Thus among South American Indians it was the custom to make an image of the god in dough and to consume it.

. . . .

This brings us back to the point from which we started. Enough has been said in this short survey of early conditions to show how intensely sacramental were men's ideas of their relationship with the unseen world. We shall take up the story of Old Testament religion in the next chapter, but in the meantime there are some remarks of a general nature that should be made.

[1] *Report of Anglo-Catholic Congress* (1927), pp. 61, 62.

PRIMITIVE IDEAS AND CUSTOMS 11

In the first place, one who is in sympathy with modern sacramental ideas must disclaim any feeling of embarrassment on account of what must appear to many the lowly ancestry of his faith.

'In the eyes of anthropologists,' it has been said, 'the Christian sacraments are interesting survivals in the modern world of primitive religious rites of initiation and communion, but happily shorn of those terrible and repulsive practices and convictions originally associated with them. Though the horrors of primitive sacrifice are absent, their symbolism is preserved in the sacraments, and so they linger with us like some ancient parish cross at which indeed few modern Englishmen kneel, but which our cultured classes view with feelings more akin to curiosity than reverence.'[1] But whatever may be true of the anthropologist and the person of modern culture, for the sincere Christian the Cross has more than all its ancient power. Christ's association with it gave it a new meaning, so that it sheds a light over the long history of suffering and self-sacrifice. So far from being emptied of significance by the passage of time, its content has become richer with each fresh act in the drama of public and private calamity. Thus it affords us an even more illuminating parallel to the history of sacramentalism than the author of the above quotation intended. It is not simply that one judges the value of a development by its end rather than by its beginning, but there is a positive pleasure in finding the pedigree so long. They who believe that God has never left Himself without a

[1] *Modern Churchman* (October 1926), p. 258.

12   SACRAMENTALISM

witness in the world will rejoice to find that the methods of His self-communication with which they are familiar to-day have their roots in a dim and scarcely recoverable past. It will greatly assist their belief in the divine governance of the world if they can see the same principles at work in all ages of its history.

> " The child is father of the man ;
> And I could wish my days to be
> Bound each to each by natural piety."

That is a sentiment with which the Christian cannot afford to dispense. There is quite enough that is unique in his religion : he will be glad to find that essential principles have remained true from the dawn of things.

Secondly, it is obvious that in the customs we have been considering and in the whole range of ideas surrounding them, there is much that might just as well count for magic as for religion. That is a conclusion that we must face unhesitatingly. Now the whole question of the connexion between magic and religion is one of the greatest complexity. Are we to say that religion is an improved form of magic, or that magic is a debased form of religion ? The general consensus of opinion among anthropologists seems to answer that neither statement is true, but that the two forms exist side by side, the same rite being either religious or magical according to the spirit in which it is undertaken. Sir James Frazer's attempt to prove that magic is an early stage of religion has broken down, and Dr. Astley's theory that ' magic and religion combined are of the

PRIMITIVE IDEAS AND CUSTOMS 13

essence of sacrament' is worthy of no greater credence. That which is social, which is undertaken for the good of the tribe as a whole, is religious; that which is anti-social, which is undertaken for the selfish purpose of an individual against the good of the tribe, is magical.

Here is a fruitful distinction, and the theologian may be forgiven for pressing it further. It is even better to find a distinction between religion and magic in their godward aspect than in their manward aspect. The attitude of magic towards the unseen powers cannot be better described than by P. Rehm in his *Histoire des Religions*.[1] 'Magic,' he says, 'corresponds to a vague philosophy of the world and of nature. If, in virtue of the animistic conception, all beings are endowed with feelings, with will, it is possible to obtain from them, as from beings like ourselves, the satisfaction of our desires. The "strategy of animism," then, consists *in making nature obedient*. Thanks to magic, man takes the offensive against things, or rather he becomes, as it were, the conductor of the orchestra in the great concert of spirits which hum about his ears. To produce rain, for instance, he pours out water: he gives the example and believes that he makes himself obeyed.' How different is this from the genius of religion, where, even in prayer, devotion finds its satisfaction not in any benefit received but in God. When the worshipper is seeking to bend the unseen powers to his own purposes, there is magic: when he seeks to know and to do the will of Heaven, there

[1] Pp. 6, 7.

14 SACRAMENTALISM

is religion. 'Not my will but Thine,' is the voice of religion ; 'Not Thy will but mine,' the voice of magic.[1]

It follows, then, that not rites in themselves can properly be called magical but the spirit that informs them. And this is as true of the rite, strictly so-called, as of the ceremony. Words can be bent to magical uses just as readily as actions or material objects. It is sometimes taken for granted that belief in the conveyance of spiritual power by material means is necessarily magical, and it is even assumed that this is magic *par excellence*. But that is as far as anything can be from the truth. A prayer may be every bit as magical as a sacrament, or it may be as essentially religious. In either case it will be the spiritual atmosphere pervading the exercise that will make the difference. 'The distinction, in fact, between magic and religion, as the *form* of man's relation to his environment, seems to be a matter of temperament rather than of time.'[2]

[1] Cf. Truc, *Les Sacraments*, p. 153.
[2] Cf. Marett (*E.R.E.*), 'Magic'; Lowie, 'Primitive Religion,' p. 136.

CHAPTER II

OLD TESTAMENT

WE have seen that sacramentalism was a universal type of religion in early days. It had no necessary connexion with magic, although it might be perverted to magical ends. Its real value was that it answered man's need for union with his god. Which end it served was decided by the psychological attitude of the user. If, then, sacramentalism was a perfectly legitimate element in religion we should naturally have expected to see it attaining strong development in the 'revealed religion' of the Old Testament.

But what actually do we find? To begin with, there is no doubt whatever that the kind of ideas sketched in the last chapter lie below the surface of the Hebrew Scriptures and that they crop through here and there. But it would be possible to argue that these outcroppings do not properly belong to the Old Testament religion at all. Unless we can show that they are accepted at least in principle by some of the great teachers, we should be compelled to admit that they belong only to the Semitic heathenism from which Judaism sprang, and were thrown off and left behind like worn-out garments as Israel proceeded on its progressive way.

This is, indeed, the impression given by the work of many Old Testament scholars. It is not (except in the case of one institution) that they seek definitely to prove that contemporary sacramentalism did not exist, but that attention is so steadfastly fixed upon the advancing moralism of Israelite religion that traces of sacramentalism are either not looked for or are left on one side as unimportant. The exception is the doctrine of sacrifice, about which a great deal has been written in recent years. The issues of the several controversies about this matter are still undecided, and it will, therefore, be best for us to leave what we have to say about it until we have dealt with the other evidences of sacramentalism to be found in the Old Testament.

That such evidences are not so plentiful as we should have expected in the straight line of genuine Yahwism we shall frankly admit. There is a twofold reason for this. In the first place, Israelite religious thought moved gradually away from the animism of early Semitic days to the deism of Sadducean times. And that movement received a strong impetus during and after the Exile, a period which must be regarded as normative for the development of that Law which dominates the Old Testament. As God was removed ever farther from the earth there was naturally less possibility of His communicating with men through material means. Yet, in spite of this tendency, the need for some sort of union with God was so strongly felt that the sacramental method of approach was still retained, even if paradoxically, in unexpected places.

OLD TESTAMENT

Secondly, the prophets had their own reason for not encouraging sacramental ideas. The very fact that these ideas were common to the races in the midst of whom the Hebrews made their home constituted for the prophets the strongest objection to them. At all costs they must preserve the distinctness of Israelite religion. In other instances where there was a possible threat of syncretism the prophets had taken severe measures to prevent it. Thus they broke up the kingdom rather than allow the oriental splendour of Solomon's reign to compromise the purity of their own type of worship. They emphasized in their teaching the feebleness of existence in Sheol rather than let the belief in a life after death lead to necromancy and spiritualism. They contrived that among their people the only animals offered to God should be such as are used for common food rather than permit the offering of animals from the wild to degenerate into a Semitic totemism. And, above all, it was an embodiment of their teaching in the Deuteronomic law that forbade the sacrifices at the many ' high places ' and centralized the cultus in Jerusalem. Their action, or that of the men who adopted their teaching in the legal codes, was in these instances of the most drastic character. No doubt a careful and philosophic discrimination might have distinguished between use and abuse, but they were dealing with a not very intelligent people, and a severe Puritanism was infinitely better than idolatry with all its degradation of morals and its toleration of human sacrifices. And so they were apt to take the shortest road to the elimination of all that could

18 SACRAMENTALISM

offend. It would scarcely have surprised us if they had adopted the same short and easy way with sacramentalism as a whole and had forbidden any but a purely 'spiritual' worship. But they stopped far short of that : they did not stress sacramental ideas, but they never attacked them on the ground that they were sacramental, and so they left them to survive, and that in the very heart of their religion.

We must leave till later a discussion of the prophetic attitude towards the particular institution of sacrifice. But whatever may be the conclusion arrived at in that discussion, we are safe in saying that among the prophets as among the other religious leaders of Israel a generally sacramental outlook upon life was assumed: it was taken for granted and never questioned.

This attitude, indeed, is quite fundamental in the Old Testament. For the Hebrew, Nature was the garment of God and also the instrument by which He worked. The long experience of the desert had tuned the senses of the wanderers to vibrate in harmony with the divine messages conveyed through the sights and sounds of the physical world. 'The heavens declared the glory of God and the firmament showed His handiwork.' This experience crystallized into stories that remained to show all the generations how outward and inward are but the twofold aspect of the one curve of the divine dealing. A pillar of cloud by day and of fire by night were the fitting manifestations of Yahweh's presence, just as the thunder and lightning were the appropriate setting for the presentation of the Law. In such circumstances it is little wonder that for their greatest leader earth could scarce 'stain the white radiance of eternity.'

> What Bard,
> At the height of his vision, can deem
> Of God, of the world, of the soul,
> With a plainness as near,
> As flashing as Moses felt,
> When he lay in the night by his flock
> On the starlit Arabian waste ?
> Can rise and obey
> The beck of the Spirit like him ?

To this we must attribute the characteristic Hebrew disregard of all secondary causes when God was perceived to be at work, and the reference of all phenomena direct to Him. The sound of the wind in the mulberry trees is made by the marching of His hosts,[1] and the prophets sum up the inspiration mediated by many and divers means in the terse formula, 'The Lord spake unto me, saying.' Therefore after the Chosen People arrived in the Promised Land, it was not possible long to tolerate the ascription by the Canaanites of the processes of agriculture to their Baalim, but the pious worshipper of Yahweh learnt to recognize in these things, too, the bountiful providence of the God who had led his fathers through the wilderness and had proved himself to be the ruler of this land. And if God thus manifested Himself through the outward things of the natural world it was perfectly easy to conclude that the life of fellowship with Him should be enshrined in an outward

[1] 2 Sam. v. 24.

form too. This was the justification for the subsequent elaborate cultus, and shows that the cultus was necessarily sacramental. If in later days it sometimes became so elaborate as to form a veil between man and his Maker, this was certainly not true of its beginnings, nor was it ever necessarily true, as we see from the passionate devotion to the Law, of so spiritual a writer as the author of Psalm cxix.

The truth of this view of the generally sacramental character of Old Testament religion can be demonstrated by an examination of the meaning of particular ceremonies. To such an examination we must now turn. It is not indeed contended that in any single instance shall we find a complete example of a sacrament in the modern sense of the word, but it is believed that the cumulative effect of the inquiry will be to prove the essentially sacramental presuppositions of Old Testament religion. We adduce examples of sacramentalism in all three modes of object, action, and word.

I

We notice first the custom of anointing. In early days the fat of an animal seems to have been particularly associated, like the blood, with its life. As fat has the power of penetrating other substances, it seemed easy for the worshipper, by applying it to a pillar or altar, to yield its virtue to the god who dwelt within. Similarly the invigorating effect of oil in a hot and dry climate upon the body of human beings led to the belief that by its means spiritual powers might be conveyed to individuals. Thus by the use of consecrated oil the Divine Spirit might be conveyed to specially privileged persons.

Three classes of the ministers of Yahweh are known to have been ceremonially anointed, namely, prophets (in some instances at least), priests, and kings. It was after his anointing that the divine afflatus showed its strength in the prophesying of so unlikely a subject as Saul, and similarly Elisha was to be solemnly set apart as Elijah's successor in the prophetic office by an act of anointing. To David the greatest crime that one could commit consisted in the act of treason implied in 'touching the Lord's anointed,' and it is definitely stated that when he himself was anointed to be king, the Spirit of the Lord 'came mightily upon him from that day forward.' But the most elaborate anointing (which indeed we do not find until we come to the latest code) was reserved for the priests, the ingredients of the sacred oil being carefully stated, and the use of the composition for other purposes being strictly forbidden. For the High Priest there was a double anointing, and a beautiful symbolic lesson is drawn from it in Psalm cxxxiii.

This leads to the recognition of the fact that there were definitely sacramental persons. If in general the spirit of man was 'the candle of the Lord,' and human personality was the most appropriate vehicle of divine power, it followed that there might be some who could become the special channels of such grace. This might be given with or without the mediation of anointing, and might manifest itself, when given, in various ways. It was to be seen in the strength of Samson and in the inspired eloquence of a great prophet.[1] It made an artist of Bezaleel [2] and a hero of Gideon.[3] Because such wrought in a spirit not properly their own they may with justice be described as truly sacramental persons.

Somewhat similar to the use of fat or oil in its underlying principles, though not in its effects, was the application of blood. In primitive times there seems to have been no objection to worshippers actually tasting the blood of a victim and so sharing in its life, but in Old Testament religion this was strictly forbidden, and the blood was reserved for God alone. This was not because of any relaxation of sacramental ideas but rather because of their intensification. The blood was so clearly associated with the life of the victim that it was regarded as an almost living thing, as *the* life *par excellence*. Thus the blood of Abel can be described, in a phrase that has become stereotyped, as 'crying out' from the ground for vengeance,[4] while the blood of the crucified Messiah is said by a later writer to 'speak' more nobly of mercy and forgiveness.[5] Even after the body has been slain the blood is therefore in some sense alive, and because it is the life it must be reserved for God alone.

The influence of this as it affected the theory of sacrifice will be considered later, but the effect of touching the blood falls within our present consideration. This is best seen in the ceremonial cleansing

[1] Isa. lxi. 1 ff. [2] Ex. xxxi. 3. [3] Judg. vi. 34.
[4] Gen. iv. 10. [5] Heb. xii. 24.

of a leper.[1] The blood of a slain bird is applied both to a living bird and to the patient. By this common contact a living identification is established between man and bird. The leper is then pronounced clean, and the bird is allowed to fly away, presumably carrying the disease with it. This sharing in a common character through the application of blood is to be seen also in the method of consecrating priests [2] and of inaugurating a covenant.[3] It is probable that this was also the origin of the sprinkling of the Passover blood upon the doorposts, Yahweh's people being thus identified as His, so that the destroying angel might pass them by.

With this employment of oil and blood we may also compare the use of water, though here our inquiry is somewhat complicated by the confusion between ceremonial and physical defilement. But the very confusion serves to illustrate the sacramental character of much of the use of water, the removal of an obvious uncleanness leading so naturally to the thought of the removal of a defilement that was not visible. Thus ablutions formed part of the initiation ceremonies of priests and Levites.[4] Water was used in the cleansing of a leper,[5] after contact with anything unclean,[6] after sexual defilement,[7] and in case of suspected adultery.[8] The facts that in some instances the water must be living or running water, and that in one case at least it must be mingled with

[1] Lev. xiv.   [2] Ex. xxix. 21.   [3] Ex. xxiv. 6–8.
[4] Ex. xxix. 4; Num. viii. 7.   [5] Lev. xiv. 8, 9.
[6] Lev. xi. 32; xv. 5; xvii. 15.   [7] Deut. xxiii. 11.
[8] Num. v. 11.

the ashes of a sacrifice,¹ serve to emphasize its sacramental character.

2

Of sacramental actions the best instance is to be found in the laying-on of hands. This ceremony has a long history behind it. As the hand is the instrument of power, it was very early conceived to be the means by which both God and man could convey power to another. It is well known how widely the touch of the hand has been held to convey the gift of healing; so common was this, indeed, that by a reflex process, especially potent medicines could be spoken of among the Greeks as ' the hands of God.' ² In the Old Testament ' the idea of the ceremony appears to be the solemn and deliberate appropriation of an object, coupled with its assignation to a particular purpose, by the person performing it. . . . It does seem to symbolize the transmission, or delegation of a moral character or quality, or of responsibility or authority (or of power to represent another).' ³ The word ' symbolize ' in this weighty judgment of Dr. Driver is somewhat vague. There can be little doubt that a spiritual relation was actually considered to be effected by the action. This relation varied in its consequences. Thus it might bring blessing to an individual,⁴ or the same

¹ Num. xix.
² Cf. ' Confirmation' (*S.P.C.K.*, 1926), vol. i. p. 2.
³ *Priesthood and Sacrifice* (ed. Dr. Sanday), pp. 39, 40.
⁴ Gen. xlviii. 14.

OLD TESTAMENT

effect might be produced for the whole congregation by the mere raising of the hands,[1] and for this latter effect we should compare the result of the lifting up of Moses' hands in the battle against Amalek. Or it might establish an identification between a worshipper and a sacrificial victim, so that the worshipper really gave himself in the animal offered.[2] Or it might effect a transference of guilt from a penitent to a victim, as in the case of the 'scapegoat' sent out to Azazel. Or it might effect the transference of powers or gifts to those who were being ordained to some holy function,[3] as in the case of Joshua, who by this ceremony was filled with the spirit of wisdom.[4] And, lastly, a solemn use of the same action where its sacramental implication is less clear, is to be found in its performance when one who has been guilty of some capital offence is being delivered to death.

Another sacramental action is that of circumcision, in which Schultz saw one of the two Old Testament sacraments, the Passover meal being the other. Into the origin of this ceremony we need not inquire; it is enough for our purpose to know that it formed the necessary initiation into the covenant relationship with Yahweh. It conferred a definite status upon the recipient and brought him into a definite spiritual relation with God. Like sacrifice, it became the vehicle of the noblest ideas of self-dedication, representing the offering through one bodily part of the

[1] Lev. ix. 22.   [2] Ex. xxix. 10, and frequently in P.
[3] Num. viii. 10; xxvii. 18–23.
[4] Deut. xxxiv. 9 (contr. Gaster, *E.R.E.*, 'Ordination').

26 SACRAMENTALISM

whole man to God and consecrating every element of his life. Not only the perpetuation of the race was hallowed, but the very thoughts of the heart; and the meaning of the ceremony was progressively spiritualized until it became possible to speak of being circumcised in heart, lips, ears, and eyes.[1]

A third sacramental action is to be found in the offering of incense. This might be done in two ways, by itself or in conjunction with other offerings, and in either case it must be carefully distinguished from the causing of the smoke of a sacrifice to ascend before God. When offered alone it might be burnt either on the altar or in a censer. Its use was a late arrival in Old Testament worship, the first certain instance of it being Jer. vi. 20 ('To what purpose cometh there to me frankincense from Sheba?'), but it formed an important part in the ceremonies of the Priestly Code. Its hygienic properties are obvious, but they form the lowest part of its significance. In ethnic religions, according to Robertson Smith, frankincense was regarded as sacred because it was the life-blood of a divine plant. Its introduction into Jewish religion may have come about independently, from its employment to do honour to people of rank and to guests at a feast.[2] The sacramental significance of which it was susceptible in ethnic religions was sublimated in the Old Testament to make it the symbol of prayer.[3] Among Egyptians it had already been regarded as the actual vehicle of prayer, and

[1] Deut. x. 16; xxx. 6; Lev. xxvi. 41; Jer. iv. 4.
[2] Dan. ii. 46; Deut. xxxiii. 10.
[3] Ps. cxli. 2; Rev. v. 8.

OLD TESTAMENT

that this significance was not lost in revealed religion is proved by Revelation viii. 3, 4, where the angel gives incense to the prayers of the saints and the smoke rises before God *for* the prayers. There is one passage in Numbers [1] where a definite atoning efficacy is attributed to the offering of incense. And lastly, it is not without interest that in later days it was while engaged upon this solemn act that John Hyrcanus became the subject of a striking example of telepathy and that Zacharias was made the recipient of a divine revelation.[2]

3

In considering the sacramental use of words among the Hebrews we must begin from the point where the name of a person is looked upon as being almost equivalent to the person himself. This idea receives particular emphasis where the person is God. It is well known that Yahweh, the personal name of Israel's God, was so dreadful that it could never be pronounced by the reader of the lessons, and there was a special injunction against ' taking God's name in vain.' This name as a kind of hypostatized power tended to become not so much identical as parallel with the person of God, so that it could be in itself a theophany or manifestation of His presence.[3] It could even do things on God's behalf, as in the blessing, ' The name of the God of Jacob defend thee.'

---

[1] Num. xvi. 46, 47.
[2] Josephus, *Ant.* xiii. 10. 3 ; Luke i. 9.
[3] Ex. xx. 24 ; xxiii. 21.

28   SACRAMENTALISM

Much the same might be said of any word that was spoken by the mouth of God. In Sumerian and Babylonian religions the obvious relation of a word to the breath had led to the word being regarded as almost equivalent to the spirit. And this has its echo in the Old Testament :

' By the word of the Lord were the heavens made ;
And all the host of them by the breath of His mouth.' [1]

The word thus conveyed the power by which creation was accomplished, and was indeed always capable of self-fulfilment. ' So shall My word be that goeth forth out of My mouth : it shall not return unto Me void, but it shall accomplish that which I please, and shall prosper in the thing whereto I send it.' [2]

Another instance of the sacramental use of words is to be found in blessing and cursing. It is natural for us to think of these as simple prayers for good or evil, but we must envisage a frame of mind to which the form of words was itself powerful enough to ensure the effect desired. Thus the writer of the story of Balak and Balaam evidently regards the latter's blessing and cursing as being thoroughly efficacious. So also when the patriarchs blessed their children, although God was recognized as the source of good, yet the actual formula employed did affect the destiny of him for whose benefit it was used.[3] This at once explains Esau's ' exceeding great and

---

[1] Ps. xxxiii. 6.
[2] Isa. lv. 11. Cf. power of a song to defeat the enemy (Judg. v. 12), or of a spell song to stay the sun (Josh. x. 12).
[3] Gen. xxvii. 28.

OLD TESTAMENT

bitter cry' when he realized that he had lost the firstborn's blessing. This belief in the value of a benediction led to the priestly habit of pronouncing a blessing after the morning and evening sacrifice,[1] as later it was pronounced at the close of the synagogue services.

A somewhat similar potency was ascribed by the Jews to the words of the Shema'.[2] To such an extent did they feel this that they took literally the command to wear them between the eyes, and invented phylacteries for the purpose. In this case we notice a slipping back into magical ideas, for the words were carried on the body and fastened upon the doorposts of a house in order to avert evil from the person and from the dwelling. But this is exceptional among the Jews. On the whole it is true to say that whereas in primitive religions, or at least in the magical rites so often associated with them, spells are all important, in the Old Testament the sacramental use of words has nothing like the same emphasis as that of actions and material substances. In general, the very fact that Israel thought Yahweh all-powerful made the growth of magic very difficult.[3]

Enough has now been said to show that sacramentalism has its place, although perhaps a subordinate one, in the religion of the Old Testament. We have not complicated the argument by dividing the development of that religion into its generally recognized stages, but the illustrations have been

[1] Num. vi. 22, 26.   [2] Deut. vi. 4–9.
[3] Gen. xviii. 14 ; 1 Sam. xiv. 6.

drawn from all periods, and it seems clear that a general atmosphere of sacramentalism pervades the whole history of Israelite worship. It is only as we understand this that we can be in a position to form an adequate opinion about the very important question of the meaning of sacrifice.

CHAPTER III

SACRIFICE AS SACRAMENT

WE have seen that one of the earliest ideas connected with sacrifice was that of communion, in the sense of sharing in the life of the God. Another such idea is that of a gift. Man's natural instinct is to offer something to the object of his affection or worship, and this instinct found its expression in sacrifice. Which of these two ideas, if either, can be said to be the origin of sacrifice is a question to which no agreed answer has yet been given. The enthusiasm aroused by Robertson Smith's adumbration of the 'communion' theory has sobered down in recent years, and there are many signs of a reaction in favour of the older 'gift' theory. In any case the two ideas are by no means mutually exclusive, and a sacramental view may provide the *raison d'être* of the one as of the other. It is important to remember this when we discuss the meaning of sacrifice in the Old Testament.

I

That the thought of communion is implied in the early Hebrew sacrifices admits of no doubt at all. This is recognized even by Buchanan Gray, who in his posthumous book, *Sacrifice in the Old Testament*, has left us a monumental consideration of other aspects of the subject. 'When a man slays an animal, gives *small* portions to Yahweh, but together with his friends eats the larger part himself, the whole proceeding is obviously something more than, or other than, the simple presentation of a gift to God' (p. 3).

But what was the precise nature of this communion? In early days, as we have seen, it meant sharing with the god in a common life, or in other instances the actual feeding upon the god himself. These notions were possible enough in an animistic or totemistic stage of religion, but do we find them even in the monolatrous period of Old Testament religion? S. C. Gayford says categorically, 'Every trace of the prehistoric " eating of the god " has disappeared from the Old Testament.'[1] This may be allowed to stand if it does not include such confessedly degenerate rites as those mentioned in Isaiah lxv. 4; lxvi. 17. But for the most part in the Old Testament it has been sublimated into the sharing with God in a common life. Of this there are at least ' traces ' in some of the sacrifices connected with early covenants. It is implied in the highly interesting story of the covenant with Abraham in Genesis xv., where Yahweh (accompanied by the patriarch?) passes as a flaming torch between the pieces of the sacrificial victim.[2]

It is more than probable that this conception of

[1] *Sacrifice and Priesthood*, p. 14.
[2] Cf. Jer. xxxiv. 18; Gen. xxxi. 54; xxvi. 30.

SACRIFICE AS SACRAMENT

communion finds some reflexion in that whole class of Hebrew sacrifices known as Peace-offerings, the type in which part of the victim was given to God by being burnt upon the altar and the rest shared between priest and offerer. But as time went on it seems that the emphasis shifted until it rested not on the thing shared but upon the fact of presence at a common board. The fundamental element in the communion would then be not the partaking of the actual life of God nor the sharing with Him in some common life, but the fellowship engendered by presence together at the sacred banquet. To eat with another implies friendship with him—at the lowest one must be on friendly terms with one's fellow-guests—and so friendship is maintained with God, who deigns thus to show His kindly recognition of those who would feast with Him. This method of communion is practised when Moses and the Seventy Elders appear before the sapphire throne of God and eat and drink in His presence,[1] and when Yahweh or His ' angel ' deigns to eat of the flesh food prepared for Him by the person whom He is visiting.[2] A later instance of it is to be seen on the occasion when Hannah chose a sacrificial meal as the most appropriate time at which to proffer her request for a son, thus giving evidence of her belief in the reality of the communion with deity that could be enjoyed through sacrifice.[3]

[1] Ex. xxiv. 9–11.
[2] Gen. xviii. ; Judg. vi. 13.
[3] 1 Sam. i. 9.

2

If fellowship is, or becomes, in this manner the sacramental significance of the peace-offering, what is to be said of those other offerings of which no part is given to the offerer? Among these there are two main classes to be distinguished—the Burnt-offering, in which the whole is consumed upon the altar, and the Sin- and Trespass-offerings of which part is burnt upon the altar and part given to the priest.

Of the former we may say at once that it lends more support to the 'gift' theory than does either of the others. Not only does it share with the others the distinctive feature of all Old Testament sacrifice, namely, that of being solemnly presented by the offerer, but also its own peculiar feature was that after the solemn presentation the whole of it was given to God by being burnt upon the altar. But even so it may be doubted whether it was ever regarded as being so simple a thing as a gift and nothing more. In primitive days, as we have seen, the object of the gift was to nourish the deity. 'The gods,' says Dr. Goudge, 'like ourselves, faint and grow weary; if "the twilight of the gods" is not to fall, they must be invigorated with food, and above all with blood, in which is the essence of life. Did the people of Yahweh, or Jehovah, ever so conceive of sacrifice? Undoubtedly. Yahweh smells the sweet savour of the sacrifice of Noah; flesh, meal, wine, and broth are offered to Him as well as blood;

SACRIFICE AS SACRAMENT

in the Old Testament " the Lord's table " does not mean the table from which God feeds man, but that from which man feeds God.'[1] On some occasions it was a means of expressing thankfulness,[2] while on others it was dictated by a lively sense of favours to come, for example, at the beginning of a war,[3] or by a desire to propitiate the deity at a particularly awe-inspiring moment.[4] These are its early associations. In later days it was the natural means of giving God the honour due to His Name, and therefore became the customary morning and evening sacrifice of the whole people.

As a gift it was in early days thought to give God pleasure because ' the food actually reached Him in the form of the fragrant fire-distilled essence,'[5] but by the time of Deuteronomy it was already regarded rather as an opportunity of giving back to God something of His own, and so recognizing the goodness of His bounty. In the later codes a still higher thought comes in and is expressed in the ceremonial. When a worshipper brings his animal to the altar, he must, before slaying it, solemnly lay his hands upon it, so identifying it with himself. Thus expression is given to the belief in the possibility of a complete self-surrender to the will of God.[6] The rationale of the sacrifice is, therefore, still sacramental. It conveys to the Divine Majesty the best gift a man has to bestow

[1] *Anglo-Catholic Congress Report* (1927), pp. 69, 70.
[2] Gen. viii. 20.
[3] Judg. vi. 26.
[4] Gen. xxii. 13 ; Judg. xiii. 16.
[5] Gen. viii. 21 ; cf. *H.D.B.* iv. 334.
[6] Lev. i. 4.

—the gift of himself. One is reminded of Christina Rossetti's Christmas hymn:

> What can I give Him
> Poor as I am?
> If I were a shepherd
> I would bring a lamb:
> If I were a wise man
> I would do my part;
> Yet what I can I give Him—
> Give my heart.

3

The gift idea was thus many-sided. It had affinities with the ideas of communion and fellowship, and it also reached out to those of expiation and propitiation. It is these latter ideas that found a more complete expression in the remaining class of sacrifices.

Sin- and Trespass-offerings do not seem to have had a definite place in Hebrew worship before the Exile. But during that period they were probably developed in priestly circles under the influence of Ezekiel. In the days of gloom and remorse that followed the fall of Jerusalem it was natural that sin and the means of escape from it should occupy an increasing space in the thoughts of the people. It is as a consequence of this that propitiation has become the most prominent feature in the final Old Testament scheme of sacrifice.

Of the two species it was the second, the Guilt- or Trespass-offering that was used when the rights of another person, God or man, had been invaded. The extent of the damage was estimated and paid

SACRIFICE AS SACRAMENT

for, and then the sacrifice was offered. In the case of the sin-offering no previous compensation was possible. The offences that were 'covered,' 'wiped away,' 'made white,' or simply 'atoned for' (whichever be the correct meaning of the Hebrew word employed in this connexion) were the unintentional offences against the ceremonial or moral law. A recent writer [1] sees a certain divine irony in the fact that the highest atoning sacrifice in the Old Testament was thus appointed for sins that were not sins at all. So, says he, the Chosen People were taught that it was impossible for the blood of bulls and goats to take away sins, and that the perfect sacrifice was still to come.

But in the meantime ideas of the greatest spiritual value were preserved in the expiatory sacrifices. The terrible nature of sin was recognized, and steps were taken for the removal of its guilt. On the other hand, the propitiatory element, the reconciling of an offended God, is more obvious in the earlier post-exilic examples than in the later instances of this type.[2] But even so it is always made clear that fellowship with God can only be restored by man's gift. And the true nature of the gift was amply revealed. The identification of the offerer with his victim by the laying on of hands, the identification of the blood with the life and its strict reservation to God alone, all alike made it clear that the worshipper was offering himself, and himself at his best, purified, as it were, by death and by fire.

[1] Gayford, *Sacrifice and Priesthood*, p. 48.
[2] Buchanan Gray, op. cit. 82 ff.

88 SACRAMENTALISM

This is the real point of the system, and it is emphasized even more strongly in the complicated ceremonies of the Day of Atonement. It would be a gross misunderstanding to think that the centre of the ritual was the offering of victims to appease an angry deity. What is really taught is that God wants man, and the inward and spiritual grace of the whole system is the offering and reception of man in a state of ideal perfection. If we are to offer ourselves to God at all, we dare only do so when every blemish has been done away.

4

There are two particular institutions in connexion with which sacrifice was offered that need especial mention because of their later association with the Christian Eucharist. These are the Passover and the ratification of a covenant. The Passover was the annual spring festival of the Hebrews, and it included three distinct features—the Paschal meal, the festival of unleavened bread, and the offering of the barley sheaf. The first of these certainly goes back to the nomadic period of Hebrew history, and as it very definitely associates a meal with a sacrifice, it points clearly to that idea of communion which we have seen to form so important an element in Old Testament worship. An interesting point arises out of the method adopted to dispose of the victim's blood. The original practice was to apply the blood outside the closed door of the house, and the object of this is expressly stated to have been the preven-

SACRIFICE AS SACRAMENT

tion of evil from entering within.[1] But the later custom, in the days when the victim was by rule slain in the Temple at Jerusalem, was to empty the blood at the base of the altar; and this may point to the incorporation of the gift idea into what was essentially a meal. But it is still the meal that is the prominent feature of the festival, and 'to eat the Passover' is a sufficient description of it throughout the New Testament. The meal was a sacred meal because its main ingredient was a sacrificial victim, and it was therefore preceded by a fast. Of the interesting questions associated with the type of victim used, and with its accompaniment of unleavened bread and bitter herbs, we need not speak. But in view of what will have to be said later, it is worth while noticing that the cups of wine that form so important a part of the meal in New Testament times were of late introduction and were probably due to Hellenistic influence.[2]

The other type of sacrifice with which the Christian Eucharist is specially associated is that offered in ratification of a covenant. 'The New Covenant in My Blood' is best understood by reference to such a scene as was enacted at Sinai (Ex. xxiv. 4–8) when Moses 'built an altar under the mountain . . . and sent the young men of the children of Israel, and they offered up burnt-offerings and sacrificed as peace-offerings bullocks to Yahweh.' On this occasion Moses took half the blood in basins and tossed it upon the altar, and the other half he tossed upon

[1] *The Destroyer*, Ex. xii. 23.
[2] Buchanan Gray, op. cit. 374, 375.

40 SACRAMENTALISM

the people, and said, 'Behold the blood of the covenant which Yahweh hath made with you upon all these conditions.' Here, apart from the communion expressed in the peace-offerings, there is the very definite association of the two parties to the covenant in the common life conveyed by the blood of the victim. The agreement was ratified by the most solemn bond known at the period.

. . . .

Ideas connected with the blood of the sacrifice have thus gone through a long process of development since the days when the early Semites partook of it freely and felt themselves sharing in the life of their God. The growing prominence of the gift idea helped to rob them of this privilege. The belief that the blood was the seat of life made it seem right to reserve that for God alone. Yet the idea of union with God to which the old usage had ministered so powerfully was preserved in the memory of the covenant sacrifices and was actually renewed in the habit of touching the offerer with the blood, while that very life-blood, so clearly identified as the offerer's own life, was itself consecrated in the act of offering by its contact with the altar and the mercy-seat, the places of God's abiding presence. This traffic in the sacramental blood established between God and His worshipper a true communion and fellowship. When we are told by a Nonconformist divine that ' the " atonement " made consists in the restoration of a quasi-physical relationship, rather than in the forensic conceptions of Protestant theology,'[1] everything we know of the general atmosphere in which Old Testament worship grew will compel us to agree.

There is a rather pathetic lack of humour in Buchanan Gray's repeated suggestion that the significance of sacrifice gradually changed and faded out of memory till at last it became a mere *opus operatum*, a thing done for the doing's sake, no one knowing why. We shall have occasion to see later in what a limited sense this is true. But we may notice now that there have always been people who perform their religious duties in that spirit : ministers of religion still castigate them from the pulpit every week. We may even find occasional justification for such a spirit : there are times when the soul, perplexed and baffled in its search for truth, may well fall back on what it believes to be the simple divine command, 'Do this.' There is a famous instance in the lines ascribed to Queen Elizabeth on the use of the sacrament of the altar :

> He took the bread and brake it,
> He was the Word that spake it,
> And what that Word doth make it,
> I do believe and take It.

But that there ever was a time when the bulk of Jewish believers had no explanation whatever to give of their rich and varied Law is simply incredible.

Nor can we whole-heartedly accept Gayford's

[1] Wheeler Robinson, *Religious Ideas of Old Testament*, p. 146 ; cf. Lev. xvii. 11.

statement that none of the Old Testament sacrifices had any grace-giving power. Their function, he says, was either to express some present feeling of the worshippers or to atone for past sin, but they could give no power for the future.[1] Of course that is true enough if we use the word in the complete sense of the grace and truth which came to believers by Jesus Christ. But if there is any power in the knowledge of restored fellowship with God, then that surely is the inward and spiritual grace of Old Testament sacrifice. However thoughtless the worshippers may have been, however regardless of the spiritual truth behind the outward form, however forgetful of the teaching of their greatest leaders, it is hard to believe that the bulk of them did not grasp and retain that fact. They may have turned aside from the thought of a quasi-physical sharing in the life of their God, but the very command that they should not appear before Him empty [2] must have assured them that at least He was there, and have guaranteed a clear emphasis upon His 'real presence' at the sacrifice. Schultz,[3] indeed, contends that 'the one really essential point in the whole ceremony of sacrifice is the confession of sin,' but it is abundantly evident that such confession is only with a view to renewed fellowship. In this sense it is possible to endorse Dr. Darwell Stone's aphorism, that in the Old Testament 'the altar of propitiation was the table of communion.'[4]

[1] Op. cit. p. 55.
[2] Isa. i. 12.   [3] *Old Testament Theology*, ii. 100.
[4] *Doctrine of Holy Eucharist*, i. 3.

SACRIFICE AS SACRAMENT

Our conclusion, then, is that sacrifice is still in the Old Testament a sacramental institution. No doubt there has been a change from the ideas of earlier days. Except in the case of the blood and the fat, the mode of sacramental transference of vital power is less by means of objects than of actions. The emphasis *tends* to shift towards a point of view in which it is no longer through the victim eaten or offered but by the performance of the whole rite that communion with God is maintained or fellowship with Him re-established. Thus, although it is not strictly accurate to say with a recent writer that ' the ceremonial is fixed ' (for, as we have seen, certain ceremonies were added to the Passover), yet it is perfectly right to continue, as that writer does, 'The meaning is fluid and progressive. The law of sacrifice says, "This do," not "this think," and the path of progress lies not only in the abolition of what is meaningless or degrading, but in putting a better meaning upon what is retained. The same ceremonial may be differently understood in one age and in another, and even in the same age by the more carnal mind and by the more spiritual. If we may not interpret differently there can be no common worship.' [1]

We must now see how the prophetic attitude towards sacrifice helped in this re-interpretation.

[1] Goudge, *Report of A.C. Congress*, p. 69.

CHAPTER IV

THE HEBREW PROPHETS

BEFORE we proceed further in our attempt to trace out the development of sacramental ideas, it is fitting that we should pause for a moment to examine the prophetic attitude towards the sacrificial system, a difficult question to which we have already made a passing reference. The close connexion that has always existed between sacrifice and sacrament makes the discussion germane to our main purpose. It will help us also to form a more definite opinion upon that other vexed question : whether the prophets found any essential opposition between such ideas as underlie the terms ' sacramental ' and ' spiritual.'

It is sometimes held that the prophets wished to put an end to the whole system of sacrifice, and a number of passages are quoted to show that they derided the belief that such offerings could be pleasing to Yahweh or effectual with Him. These should be read at length, and it is particularly important that they should be studied in the light of their context. They are :

1. ' Come to Beth-el, and transgress ; to Gilgal, and multiply transgression ; and bring your sacrifices every morning, and your tithes every three days ;

and offer a sacrifice of thanksgiving of that which is leavened, and proclaim freewill offerings and publish them: for this liketh you, O ye children of Israel, saith the Lord God' (Amos iv. 4, 5).

2. 'Shall not the day of the Lord be darkness, and not light? even very dark, and no brightness in it? I hate, I despise your feasts, and I will take no delight in your solemn assemblies. Yea, though ye offer me your burnt-offerings and meal-offerings, I will not accept them; neither will I regard the peace-offerings of your fat beasts. Take thou away from me the noise of thy songs; for I will not hear the melody of thy viols. But let judgement roll down as waters, and righteousness as a mighty stream. Did ye bring unto me sacrifices and offerings in the wilderness forty years, O house of Israel? Yea, ye have borne Siccuth your king and Chiun your images, the star of your god, which ye made to yourselves. Therefore will I cause you to go into captivity beyond Damascus, saith the Lord, whose name is the God of hosts' (Amos v. 20–27).

3. 'O Ephraim, what shall I do unto thee? O Judah, what shall I do unto thee? for your goodness is as a morning cloud, and as the dew that goeth early away. Therefore have I hewed them by the prophets. I have slain them by the words of my mouth: and thy judgements are as the light that goeth forth. For I desire mercy, and not sacrifice; and the knowledge of God more than burnt-offerings' (Hos. vi. 4–6).

4. 'Hear the word of the Lord, ye rulers of Sodom; give ear unto the law of our God, ye people of Gomorrah. To what purpose is the multitude of your sacrifices unto me? saith the Lord: I am full of the burnt-offerings of rams, and the fat of fed beasts; and I delight not in the blood of bullocks, or of lambs, or of he-goats. When ye come to appear before me, who hath required this at your hand, to

trample my courts ? Bring no more vain oblations ; incense is an abomination unto me ; new moon and sabbath, the calling of assemblies—I cannot away with iniquity and the solemn meeting. Your new moons and your appointed feasts my soul hateth : they are a trouble unto me ; I am weary to bear them. And when ye spread forth your hands, I will hide mine eyes from you : yea, when ye make many prayers, I will not hear : your hands are full of blood. Wash you, make you clean ; put away the evil of your doings before from mine eyes ; cease to do evil ; learn to do well ; seek judgement, relieve the oppressed, judge the fatherless, plead for the widow ' (Isa. i. 10–17).

5. ' O my people, remember now what Balak king of Moab consulted, and what Balaam the son of Beor answered him ; remember from Shittim unto Gilgal, that ye may know the righteous acts of the Lord. Wherewith shall I come before the Lord, and bow myself before the high God ? shall I come before him with burnt-offerings, with calves of a year old ? Will the Lord be pleased with thousands of rams, or with ten thousands of rivers of oil ? shall I give my firstborn for my transgression, the fruit of my body for the sin of my soul ? He hath shewed thee, O man, what is good ; and what doth the Lord require of thee, but to do justly, and to love mercy, and to walk humbly with thy God ? ' (Mic. vi. 5–8).

6. ' Thus saith the Lord of hosts, the God of Israel : Add your burnt-offerings unto your sacrifices, and eat ye flesh. For I spake not unto your fathers, nor commanded them in the day that I brought them out of the land of Egypt, concerning burnt-offerings or sacrifices ; but this thing I commanded them, saying, ' Hearken unto my voice, and I will be your God, and ye shall be my people : and walk ye in all the way that I command you, that it may be well with you ' (Jer. vii. 21–23).

THE HEBREW PROPHETS 47

Comparison should also be made with Psalms xl. 6–8; li. 7, 16–19.

It will be seen at once that by isolating some sections of these passages from their context a good case could be made out for believing that the prophets did repudiate the whole sacrificial system, and it is no doubt by some such unconscious isolation that the prophetic aloofness has come to be grossly exaggerated. But an examination of the passages as a whole makes it clear that if sacrifice is repudiated then a good deal more must go with it. Not only all days of special observance, including the Sabbath, must go, but also the habit of frequenting the Temple, and even fasting and the offering of prayer. But this would be a *reductio ad absurdum* of the whole prophetic teaching. No doubt the prophets feel that the cultus has usurped too large a place in the popular religion; hence the reference of Amos and Jeremiah to the small part played by sacrifice in the desert wanderings, and Isaiah's apparent questioning of the force of the regulation, ' Ye shall not see My face empty-handed.'[1] But it is by no means clear that they wished to stand apart from the organized religion that they knew so well. Thus Samuel shares in sacrifice, Elijah mourns the loss of the old sanctuaries, Amos preaches at the Bethel shrine, Hosea[2] regards loss of sacrifice as a public calamity, Isaiah is worshipping in the Temple when he sees his great vision, and he looks forward to a time when even the Egyptian shall bring sacrifice to Yahweh, Deuteronomy is an endeavour to embody

[1] Isa. i. 12.   [2] Hos. iii. 4.

48 SACRAMENTALISM

prophetic teaching in a cult, Jeremiah is himself a priest who regards a multitude of sacrifices as a most joyful part of the worship of the future,[1] Ezekiel is another priest who frames an ideal cultus, the great prophet of the Exile can only express the most idealistic form of religious devotion under sacrificial symbolism,[2] and the very psalm that speaks most strongly of God's lack of delight in sacrifice reveals its own origin in the cultural act of purging with hyssop, a primitive 'asperges.'[3] With the Exile indeed there had come a great longing for the restoration of the cultus and many attempts to frame it on new and ideal lines. It was natural, therefore, that after the Return the prophets should be the most eager to urge on the rebuilding of the Temple, and that people like Haggai and Zechariah should promise in God's name an era of abundant blessing when once the worship had been restored.

We have then two apparently contradictory elements in the prophetic teaching, and the effort to effect a formal reconciliation between them seems likely to be unavailing. The best recent discussion of the question is to be found in Dr. Skinner's very careful consideration of the relation of Jeremiah to the Deuteronomic law, and this may be taken as a test case for the whole matter.[4]

In spite of vigorous attacks upon the position we may still, he says, believe that the Deuteronomic reformation took place under Josiah, while Jeremiah

[1] Jer. xvii. 26; xxxiii. 18.   [2] Isa. liii.
[3] Ps. li. See Simpson, *Psalmists*, p. 11.
[4] Skinner, *Prophecy and Religion*, pp. 106 *et passim*.

was yet a little known prophet, living quietly at Anathoth, and that he was an eye-witness of this effort to purify contemporary worship by withdrawing all sacrifice from the country shrines and forbidding its practice outside Jerusalem. At first Jeremiah whole-heartedly supported the scheme, and if he had retained this attitude of appreciation our task would have been simple. But in the result he seems to have been disillusioned. ' Very soon its defects became apparent : its superficiality, its inability to cope with prevalent immorality, and the surviving tendencies to polytheism and superstition ; and Jeremiah began to suspect the inherent impotence of the legal method of dealing with national sin. At a later time he detected a worse evil in the new-born spirit of self-righteousness based on a formal acceptance of the Covenant and an outward compliance with its demands.' It has been suggested that this put him out of sympathy altogether with any outward cultus and especially with that part of it which included sacrifice. ' But we need not suppose that Jeremiah, any more than Jesus and Paul, repudiated the law which was the occasion of this evil, as in itself of no authority. And in spite of differences there are close affinities between the school of Deuteronomy and the teaching of Jeremiah. The mere fact that the prophecies of Jeremiah were edited by the Deuteronomic school shows that there was no consciousness of antagonism between them.'

It ought to be obvious that one who stood in this sort of relation to Deuteronomy could not well have desired the total abolition of sacrifice. Yet it is certainly true that just as Jeremiah's insistence on the need of a personal religion loosened the foundations of the old national conception of religion, so his insistence on the need of a direct inward relation between the soul and God helped to undermine the conception of sacrifice as a necessary and exclusive means of approach to God. In the popular view sacrifice was the chief and indispensable means of maintaining intercourse between God and man. Many of the prophets, however, foresaw a condition of things in which the Temple would be destroyed and sacrifice would consequently be impossible, and they were providentially guided to adumbrate a method of fellowship with God which should not be mediated by sacrifice. But Dr. Skinner goes too far when he maintains that they were therefore led to hold up to their contemporaries the ideal of a religion wholly based on moral fellowship between God and man, 'in which sacrificial worship was at best an irrelevance, and at worst an offence.' We must not allow ourselves to fall into the old fallacy of trying to build up a complete system of theology on a few proof texts, and we must balance the righteous impatience of the passages cited, which are after all comparatively rare in proportion to the whole bulk of prophecy, with the acceptance of sacrifice implied in the rest of prophetic teaching. The question we have to ask is : What was the attitude of the prophets to religious institutions as they saw them, not in some vision of the future, but in the actual practice of their own day ?

We shall not be far wrong if we answer that what

the prophets wished to do was not to abolish but to reform it. If their language seems rather exaggerated for the purpose we must remember that in no age have preachers found themselves able to use measured terms in their denunciation of abuses. The tendency to run to extremes would receive a special emphasis in a day when theology was not so exact a science even as it is now. That we are justified in such a judgment becomes still more probable when we discover the precise objects of the prophetic attack. These were two : materialism and idolatry.

The first of these is the failing that must always be the peculiar danger of any sacramental system ; it is so much easier to rest content with the outward than to penetrate to the inward. In the case of sacrifice there was a particular temptation to this because of the accompanying feast. The prophets allege that the worshippers are more prone to remember that the sacrifice is agreeable to themselves than that it is agreeable to Yahweh.[1] This shows that the prophets are thinking especially of the peace-offering, and it explains why they so often denounce excesses that accompany religious banquets.[2] But even gift-sacrifices are not free from abuse, and an especial attack is directed against the theory that God can be influenced by the number and splendour of such gifts.[3] What is more important than the gift is the moral standing of the offerer. The prophets are never tired of pointing out that worship without righteousness is an insult to God. Their whole teach-

[1] Amos iv. 5. [2] Amos ii. 7 ; Hos. iv. 13.
[3] Ezek. xx. 28.

ing is a grand attack upon the theory that the favour of Yahweh can be won by the maintenance of a cultus without any corresponding effort after holiness of life.

That theory was particularly prominent among the heathen. And that is the chief reason why the prophets spend so much force in the denunciation of idolatry and of any association with the ceremonies of the surrounding nations. Thus, what Micah opposes in the famous passage (vi. 1-8) is not sacrifice in itself but the essentially magical theory of sacrifice that impels Balak to offer holocausts in the hope of encompassing the ruin of Israel.

Such heathen theories led also to the offering of human sacrifice denounced in the same passage of Micah.[1] Other associated practices condemned as idolatrous are offerings to the dead,[2] and feasts in which many animals forbidden to the Hebrew played a part.[3] Robertson Smith points out[4] that these sacred meals represent a reversion to primitive totemistic type in days when it was believed that Yahweh had forsaken His land,[5] that they became common at about the same period in Assyria and Babylon, that they were the precursors of the mystery cults which became so important at a later day, and that in distinction from their rapid spread among other peoples they were actually held in check among the Jews by the strong opposition of the law and prophets. It will be seen, therefore, that the prophetic

[1] Cf. Ezek. xx. 31.
[2] Ps. cvi. 28.
[3] Ezek. viii. 10; Isa. lxv. 4; lxvi. 17.
[4] *Religion of the Semites*, pp. 357 f.
[5] Ezek. viii. 12.

THE HEBREW PROPHETS

criticisms of the cultus must be read by the light not only of a prevailing sacramentalism but also of a continual threat of returning idolatry. It might, indeed, be asked whether there is not some necessary connexion between sacramentalism and idolatry, and it is certainly worth while asking what idolatry meant to the prophets.

Of the class of objects covered by the term 'idols' three species are to be distinguished. The first is the talisman, which is simply a material object believed to possess magical power. The second is the fetish, which is a shaped object, generally in the form of some animal, believed to be inhabited by a spirit. And the third is the idol proper—shaped in human form and indwelt by the spirit of the god. It is probable that all these played their part in the primitive religion of the ancestors of Israel.[1] In any case we have sufficient evidence that they were a constant source of temptation to the Hebrews of Old Testament times.

That temptation expressed itself in two ways: it drove them repeatedly towards heathen worship and it led them to introduce idols into the worship of Yahweh. The first tendency came out strongly in the time of the Judges, of Solomon, and of Manasseh. The second was first denounced as evil by Hosea,[2] and was the chief object of attack in the drastic reforms of Hezekiah and Josiah. The two tendencies blended easily enough together, and formed a large element in that danger of syncretism with the religion of the surrounding nations that gave rise

[1] Josh. xxiv. 2. [2] Hos. viii. 5, 6; x. 5.

54 SACRAMENTALISM

to such grave anxieties throughout the course of Hebrew history to the Exile, and led to the erection of the protective barrier of the Law afterwards.

Idolatry in the Biblical sense is thus seen to be either apostasy from Yahweh or a debased sacramentalism that 'forgot the tenant while remembering the tenement.' Against it in both forms the prophets set themselves with all their force, and in order to eradicate the last relics of it the later prophets forbade the use of any image, the Brazen Serpent whose healing spirit was under the control of Yahweh no less than the Bull Calves which were the abodes of the spirit of Yahweh Himself. But this was also the standpoint of the Law, and the Law, as we have seen, contained a host of sacramental forms. We may conclude, therefore, that the prophets were no more opposed to a *pure* sacramentalism than they were to pure offerings.

An interesting corroboration of this view has recently come to light through such researches as those of Dr. Wheeler Robinson into the meaning of prophetic symbolism. The mimetic and other symbolic actions of the prophets have long been regarded as a sort of 'acted parable,' illustrations in action of the teaching given by word. But it is a serious question whether in the mind of the prophet they were not much more than that. It seems likely that they were thought actually to assist in bringing about that which they signified. Thus Elijah, by stretching himself upon the dead boy and then rising and walking to and fro, actually helped the boy to do the same. Elisha, by commanding the king to strike

THE HEBREW PROPHETS 55

the arrows on the ground, was not simply indulging in some form of rhabdomancy, but actually striking blows at his country's enemies.[1]

The likeness of this to the old ' sympathetic magic ' is too obvious to need comment. But it is not itself magic. For whereas the magician sought to constrain the supernatural forces to his will, the prophet is acting in obedience to what he believes to be the will of Yahweh. There are even occasions when the prophet is himself constrained by the divine command in performing these actions to assist in the accomplishment of a purpose, the contemplation of which moves him to a shuddering abhorrence. So when Isaiah clothes himself as a captive he assists in the furtherance of Yahweh's decree to send His people into captivity,[2] and when Jeremiah first binds on himself a new waist-cloth and then puts it off and ruins it in the mud and damp, he is, to his own exquisite agony and distress, aiding to bring about the rejection of his people at the hand of God.[3]

Thus in the mind of the very men who taught Israel the loftiest ethical idealism that was ever preached to any nation of the old world, we see evidence of that close connexion between the inward and the outward which constitutes the essence of sacramentalism. It is impossible not to recognize here an approximation to our second sacramental mode, that of action, and such recognition should

---

[1] 2 Kings xiii. 16 ff. Cf. Peake, *Commentary on Bible*, p. 308–9, and a paper by Dr. Wheeler Robinson in *Old Testament Essays*, 1927.

[2] Is. xx.   [3] Jer. xiii. 1 ff.

make us the readier to acknowledge a sacramental background to the rest of prophetic thought.

What, then, was the prophet's contribution to the development of sacramentalism ? Simply this, that they passed the sacramental ideas that were natural and indeed necessary to themselves as to their countrymen through the fine sieve [1] of their exalted ethicism. By them the cultus is made entirely subservient to the overwhelming thought of the holiness of God, and that holiness includes the loftiest moral goodness. Thus, in keeping with the genius of the Old Testament generally, that which among other nations descends to puerility or worse becomes among the Hebrews the instrument of the highest relations between God and man. So, to take but one instance, the idea of 'eating the god,' which many have believed to lie at the basis of the whole sacrificial system, became progressively purified in the religion of Israel, passing through a belief in the possibility of communion and fellowship to the offering of a will and conduct that are alike made in the image of God. And throughout the long development the logical continuity of the belief was preserved by outward and visible signs that were essentially sacramental.

Nevertheless the prophetic emphasis on the moral side of religion, reinforced by the Jews' divorce from the opportunities of practising their own cultus during the Exile, undoubtedly weakened the grasp upon the connexion between the outward and inward side of worship. Consequently, during the remaining

[1] I owe the figure to Dr. Vernon Bartlet.

THE HEBREW PROPHETS

centuries of Jewish history the interest in a sacramental view of nature is much fainter. But outside the limits of Judaism, in the world of Pagan beliefs and practice, that interest during these centuries attains a strong development which was not without its reaction upon Judaism itself. As Jevons puts it : [1] ' At times the sacramental conception of sacrifice appeared about to degenerate entirely into the gift theory ; but then in the sixth century B.C., the sacramental conception woke into new life, this time in the form of a search for a perfect sacrifice—a search which led Clement and Cyprian to try all the mysteries of Greece in vain.' It is to the history of these mysteries that we now turn.

[1] *Introduction to the History of Religion*, p. 414.

CHAPTER V

THE MYSTERY RELIGIONS

WHEN Alexander the Great in the middle of the fourth century B.C. conquered the East, the gods of Olympus had no share in his victories. The old Greek religion had already lost its hold over the minds of men, and the conquests of the soldiers only served to open the floodgates through which the religious ideas of the barbarians could pour in upon the vacant soil.

Essentially the new forms of religion were quite alien from the intellectual philosophy that had proved the crown and glory of Greek development. But a point of contact was formed by that ineradicable interest in the natural world which had always been the inspiration of philosophical speculation among the Greeks. Under eastern tuition this was translated into an emotional sympathy with the ever-recurring drama of Nature's yearly dying and rising again. There thus took place what was in some respects a reversion to the type of those primitive religious forms that have already claimed our attention. In the early stages a plant or an animal seems to have been identified with the unseen power in Nature, and by feeding upon it the worshippers felt themselves to be united with the life-principle, eternal and

THE MYSTERY RELIGIONS 59

invincible, that was contained within and expressed by these outward embodiments. Later, some god or hero of mythology took the place of the plant or animal, and elaborate ceremonies re-enacted his ' passion,' which was in effect a dramatization of the death of vegetation in winter and its restoration to life in the spring.

The earliest known form of this kind of worship was the cult of Dionysus, the son of Zeus and Semele, who, in the form of a bull, was rent asunder and eaten by the Titans. His heart, however, was rescued and swallowed by Zeus, and from him Dionysus was re-born. This cult was celebrated in Thrace, before the sixth century B.C., with Bacchanalian orgies and the rending and eating of a bull. During that century an advance took place when the worship of Dionysus was crossed with that of Orpheus. This hero was fabled to have entered the underworld and rescued his wife from the shades, only to lose her again, and then to have been himself torn to pieces by the Thracian women whose advances he had rejected. In the resulting amalgamation of these two cults the cruder excesses of the Dionysiac worship disappeared; unity with the god was now sought not so much by Bacchic frenzy as by spiritual ecstasy. In the fourth century communities are found practising this Orphic worship with imposing ceremonies and rites of initiation, demanding a measure of asceticism on the part of would-be initiates, and guaranteeing them immortality as the reward of participation.

Gradually other conceptions came to colour the

religious atmosphere and to define more clearly both the hopes and fears of men, and consequently to enrich the possibilities offered by the mystery cults. Under the influence of Stoicism the many gods of Olympus became regarded as personifications of one Supreme Being. Persian thought in a somewhat similar way hypostatized the forces of the natural world and made them dependent upon an ultimate reality, just as in later days Gnosticism was to personify the attributes of God and make them into emanations from Him. Human life was not under the immediate control of the Supreme Being, but of Allotted Destiny, the inexorable functions of which were performed for the Persians by the Seven Planetary Rulers. It was under the bondage of this death that men groaned and from which the mysteries offered them some means of escape. For in the cult they were united with a hero or god who had triumphed over death. Thus closely associated with him they might themselves make good their escape out of the prison-house of fate and mortality into a sphere within the protection of the Supreme.

This seems to have been the general rationale of the Mystery Religions. It is evidence of an underlying principle of unity that made for a considerable measure of toleration among the cults. But we must not conclude that the syncretism was thoroughgoing, and that there existed, as some have imagined, a kind of universal amalgamated religion. The several cults lived on side by side ; they never really fused, but the aim in each case was the same and

THE MYSTERY RELIGIONS 61

the methods employed seem to have been similar. But the documentary evidence is scarce, difficult to date, and not always easy to interpret. However, we know something of the four main cults belonging to the general type already outlined.

I

The first is that of the famous Eleusinian mysteries, which were celebrated in honour of Demeter and Persephone and became the state religion of Athens. Orphic influence came in through the identification of Dionysus with Iacchus, the son of Persephone; and there is an obvious similarity between the story of Orpheus' wife and that of the abduction of Persephone by the king of the underworld and her return to the upper air with the blossoms and flowers at the spring of the year. It is therefore probable that the main effort of the cult was to establish a union between the worshippers and the divine hero of the conflict with death by means of a 'passion-play' or tableau which represented the adventures of the god.

Three elements may be distinguished in the rites of initiation. First, there was a period of purification. This was followed by an exhortation, which may have taught magical formulae or explained the meaning of mystic actions. Finally there came the 'epopteia,' or vision of sacred scenes, which manifested the glory of the deities. This last was the culminating point in the mysteries and was designed to produce so strong an emotional reaction in the

62   SACRAMENTALISM

participant as to give the sense of union with the divine life, and thus to effect both a change in moral character and an emancipation from the fear of death. We may compare with this the Christian 'beatific vision,' which, according to S. John will change the beholder into something like God Himself. It is possible that this feeling was strengthened in sacramental fashion by the drinking of a sacred potion. Clement of Alexandria mentions [1] a *kykeon* or barley-drink taken at the end of the initiatory fast. It has been conjectured that this was done in memory of the barley-drink with which Demeter broke her fast of mourning for Persephone, and if this is correct the action would no doubt intensify the feeling of union with the goddess.

2

The next of the cults is that of the Great Mother Cybele, which was native to Phrygia, but was brought to Rome as the result of a special embassy in 204 B.C. during the war with Carthage. The great festival of this cult took place in the spring, and recalled the tragedy of the youth Attis, who, in remorse for his infidelity towards his goddess-lover, mutilated himself beneath a pine tree. In the ceremonies a pine tree was cut down, treated as a corpse, and buried. Afterwards the grave was opened and the announcement made that the god still lived. This was followed by a carnival which was no doubt largely influenced by the Dionysus cult. It seems

[1] *Protrept.* ii. 21.

to have included some sort of sacramental meal, for a formula has been preserved which contains the words, ' From the tympanum I have eaten ; from the cymbal have I drunk : I am become an initiate of Attis.' By the middle of the second century A.D. there had also been introduced into this cult a kind of baptism in the blood of a bull, called ' taurobolium.' An interesting inscription still survives which describes those who have undergone this baptism as ' for ever born again.' The day on which the rite was performed was called their spiritual birthday (Natalicium).[1]

3

The third of the mystery cults is that of Isis, which originated in Egypt, and then spread through the Empire in the second century B.C. The myth tells how Osiris, the husband and brother of Isis, was put to death and cut in pieces by Set. Isis, after long and painful search, found the mangled remains and buried them. Thereupon Osiris became king of the underworld, but his life above-ground was renewed in his son Horus. The obvious similarity between this and the other mystery cult myths was strengthened by the ready identification of Osiris with Dionysus, and of Isis with any and all of the other goddesses of the same type.

We are fortunate in having from the pen of Apuleius a contemporary description of the demands that

[1] Halliday, *The Pagan Background of Early Christianity*, p. 264.

were made upon an applicant for initiation into the mysteries of Isis. There is a long wait in the temple, with much prayer and fasting, till the goddess herself summons him, apparently in a dream. Then on the appointed day he is led forth in procession and washed in the sacred laver. The culminating experience comes when he is admitted into the very presence of the goddess and receives mystic communications, of which, unfortunately, he must never divulge the secret. So Lucius, the hero of Apuleius, exclaims, 'I penetrated to the boundaries of death : I trod the threshold of Persephone and after being borne through all the elements I returned to earth. At midnight I beheld the sun radiating white light : I came into the presence of the gods below and the gods above, and did them reverence close at hand.'[1]

4

To these three mysteries should be added for the sake of completeness those of Mithras. But they are not really important for our purpose, for, although they were practised in Asia Minor before the beginning of the Christian era, they were not widespread until the second and third centuries A.D., and therefore can hardly have made any large contribution to that general diffusion of sacramental ideas which preceded the birth of Christianity. But it is in connexion with these mysteries that the taurobolium became best known, and it is also in connexion with them that Justin Martyr made his famous assertion

[1] Cf. Kennedy, S. *Paul and The Mystery Religions*, p. 102.

THE MYSTERY RELIGIONS 65

that the demons had invented a caricature of the Christian Eucharist. Sacred food in the shape of bread and a cup of water was used at a certain stage of the initiation. From a consideration of the dates it might well seem that Justin's allegation was correct and that this meal was indeed borrowed from the Christians, but the prevalence of somewhat similar ceremonies in other mysteries and the fact that this was part of the rites of initiation and not the practice of adepts makes any connexion appear doubtful.

What now were the features that the mystery cults possessed in common ? They were all mutually tolerant, although of course initiation into one did not involve initiation into another, and even apparently to be an adept, for instance, of the Isis cult at Alexandria would not necessarily involve recognition as such in the corresponding cult-brotherhood at Rome. But apart from that, these religions knew no barrier of race or class, and offered the right hand of fellowship even to slaves and women. This fellowship led to ' salvation.' If we ask, ' Salvation from or to what ' ? the precise answer is not always clear. But at least it included those two things most valuable in an age characterized, as Professor Gilbert Murray says, by ' failure of nerve,' namely, freedom from the pressure of a blind fear and a guarantee of immortality. This double effect of salvation was brought about by the worshipper's identification with the divine hero, an identification so close that he was often called by the name of the god. And this identification was itself brought about by sacraments of initiation and participation, and by an imposing ceremonial which led up to an overwhelming and transforming 'vision' or mystical experience.

No doubt there was a good deal of what would seem to us childish play-acting, and the sense of psychological change was produced by such doubtful means as drugged potions after a period of fasting and by sudden emergence into bright light after a time spent in total darkness. Effects thus obtained were heightened by clothing the initiate with the garments of the god and causing him to be hailed by the divine name before the assembled congregation. But all this was itself an exhibition of a crude form of sacramentalism. And the evidence for some sort of sacred eating and drinking is too plentiful to allow us to escape the general sacramental implication of the whole process. There was the barley drink at Eleusis, the eating of raw flesh in the Orphic cults, the eating from the tympanum and drinking from the cymbal in the mysteries of Attis, and the bread and water of the Mithraic mysteries. And to crown all, there is the evidence for the Isis worship afforded by an invitation from a certain Chairemon, summoning a friend to dinner 'at the table of the Lord Serapis in the Serapeum to-morrow.'[1] From all this we are forced to realize that we are dealing with a scheme of redemption, which, however crudely worked out, is essentially sacramental in character.

This is the type of religion which in the form of

[1] Grenfell and Hunt, *Oxyrhynchus Papyri*, i. 110 (cf. iii. 523).

the various cults spread throughout the Roman empire when belief in the old gods had passed away. Essentially it is unjustifiable to speak of it as one religion, but at the lowest it represents a common point of view, and there was enough cohesion about it to make it the most formidable neighbour of late Judaism and early Christianity. The question of fundamental importance that thus arises is whether the mystery cults had any profound influence on the progress of these religions.

The answer often given nowadays is that although they left Palestine itself untouched, the cults affected profoundly the character of Christianity as it passed into Asia Minor and other parts of the empire, transforming the simple ethicism of the Gospel into a new mystery cult wherein the Christ became a saviour-god who was united with His worshippers by an elaborate sacramental system. For ourselves we find this theory unsatisfactory, both in what it denies and in what it affirms. On the one hand it is impossible to regard Palestine as a country hermetically sealed against all influence from outside, and on the other it is equally impossible to see in S. Paul the kind of person who could be so easily beguiled into accepting as his own a religious system which was, *ex hypothesi*, fundamentally alien from that which he had set out to teach. The theory involves the belief that while the mystery religions were essentially sacramental, sacramentalism was of no consequence at all in late Judaism and original Christianity. Whether such a belief is justified or not we must now proceed to examine.

CHAPTER VI

THE BACKGROUND OF CHRISTIANITY

HOW far had the atmosphere of the Mystery Religions penetrated Palestine ? That is a question which it is exceedingly difficult to answer. It is often suggested, e.g. by Buchanan Gray,[1] that if there was but little sacramentalism to be found among the Chosen People during Old Testament times, there was at the period when Christianity arose none at all. Even Oesterley,[2] who is ready to allow that with the Israelites, as with the reformer John, the rite of baptism had a sacramental significance, will allow it no such meaning among the later Jews. Bousset[3] admits that this is curious, as the Mysteries all had sacraments, but contends that the Pharisaic washings had become mere legal obligations without significance, and that even the proselyte baptism was not held to produce any inner change, and concludes that ' the Jewish Church on the whole knows no sacrament.' The reason for this is summarized by Fairweather,[4] who explains that the

---

[1] Op. cit. 51 ; cf. Ecclus. xxxv. 1 ff.
[2] Oesterley and Box, *Religion and Worship of the Synagogue*, pp. 283 ff.
[3] *Religion des Judenthums* (3rd edition), p. 199.
[4] *Background of the Gospel*, p. 66.

THE BACKGROUND OF CHRISTIANITY 69

restoration of the cultus after the return from exile was not a reversion to heathen practice, because the rites were ' denaturalized and transformed into commemorative institutions of supernatural religion,' worship thus becoming a matter of simple obedience to Divine law. Instead of being a bridge between Jews and heathen as it had been before the exile, the cultus now became an effectual barrier. In short, it is held that the later religion of the elect people was denuded of all sacramental significance.

Now it is clearly possible to exaggerate this aloofness. Bertholet [1] sees many non-Jewish customs incorporated into the Priestly Code. ' The best method of making heathenism harmless was to absorb it. Even the gods of alien people had to do duty in helping to enlarge the court of Yahweh and act as His angels (Dan. x. 13, 20 ; Ps. lviii. 1 ; lxxxii. 1–6). Indeed, in all that Judaism absorbed from heathenism it saw a kind of spiritual tribute paid by other faiths to that of Yahweh ; and it received it as readily as it received at a later time those sacrifices with which foreigners did homage to the God of the Jews in the Temple at Jerusalem. In the Book of Malachi we meet the thought that all the worship in the world belongs to Yahweh (Mal. i. 11).' More guardedly Streeter [2] tells us that, ' situated as he was, the Jew could hardly help gradually absorbing and incorporating into his own religion (in a form which harmonized with its own natural development) the more valuable elements in the religion of those among

[1] *History of Hebrew Civilization*, p. 379.
[2] *Adventure*, p. 169.

whom he sojourned—not by way of conscious imitation, but of that unconscious assimilation by which living minds always appropriate from current thought whatever is congenial to their own fundamental bent. Already, as the Old Testament shows, the Jew had borrowed not a little from Babylonia—and had vastly improved it in the borrowing. So, too, without losing what his fathers had gained, he could learn from the religion of Persia and from the philosophy of Greece. From Zoroastrianism came the conceptual framework of that Apocalyptic literature which was for Judaism the source of the belief in resurrection and judgment after death. In the Book of Wisdom, and still more in Philo, we see how the Jew could learn also from the Greek—to see God, not only as the transcendent creator of the universe, but also as its immanent, all-pervading, ever-creating and sustaining spirit.'

It is true that the latter passage was written of the Jews of the Dispersion, but we suggest that it gives an admirable description of much that went on at least in certain areas of Palestine. No doubt a very different spirit characterized the Scribes and Pharisees of our Lord's day, but every one knows that popular piety underwent a process of growing detachment from the Temple and its services. It is, therefore, unsafe to argue from official to unofficial Judaism. It is known that Jews of the Dispersion could support heathen cults and even swear by an Egyptian goddess, and there is a consequent possibility that their brethren in Palestine might be much more open to foreign influences than has often been supposed. It has never yet been found easy to exclude propaganda from any country. Thought is too subtle a thing to be kept out by guards or by the fence of a law. Palestine had always been a highway between great nations. At this time pilgrims were continually pouring into Jerusalem from all quarters of the civilized world. Hellenic influence, which was even now so strongly felt at Alexandria, had centres nearer hand in Ptolemais and a host of other Greek cities, and there was the Greek language spoken everywhere.

Hellenism, indeed, had been officially encouraged by the civil government in Palestine. It is true that the ill-starred effort of Antiochus Epiphanes to force the Jews to accept the Hellenistic culture had produced a reaction against all foreign influence, but when the Romans became masters in the Holy Land the pendulum swung back again, and rulers like Aristobulus I and Alexander Jannaeus had led a new Hellenizing movement. This had culminated in the work of Herod the Great, who had actually rebuilt the Temple in the Greek style and planted a golden eagle over the Great Gate.[1]

Still deeper into the heart of Jewish worship had Hellenistic influence penetrated. The rite of the Passover itself had been enriched by the insertion of the ceremonial drinking of cups of wine. This meant the signal defeat of such ancient Hebrew influences as that of the Rechabites. And as if to assert more triumphantly the Gentile character of the innovation, the wine was not drunk pure, after the Eastern

[1] Fairweather. *Jesus and the Greeks*, pp. 221, 222.

fashion, but mixed with water, as was the custom among the Greeks and Romans.[1]

If official Judaism could accept so much, what must have been the effect on the unlettered multitude? Their ignorance or defection was so clearly recognized that the Pharisees erected as strong a barrier between themselves and the common people as that which already existed in ideal between the whole nation and the heathen. But Pharisaic aloofness only left the bulk of the people more open to outside influences. As the Mystery Religions were the cults of the vulgar rather than of the philosopher, there would be a natural affinity between the sacramentalism of the mysteries and the lingering traces of Hebrew sacramentalism.

The area in which foreign influences would meet with least resistance was Galilee—the original home of Christianity, and its natural habitat to such an extent that it has been said that 'Christianity was mainly a Galilean affair.' That the rabbis looked upon Galilee as particularly heretical is well known. 'Search and see that out of Galilee ariseth no prophet.' 'Can any good thing come out of Nazareth?' 'Galilee, Galilee, thou hatest the law, therefore thou shalt yet find employment among robbers.'[2] Archaeological research has emphasized this loose character of Galilean Judaism. There are numerous ruins of synagogues scattered about Galilee which were first discovered in 1852. Those that

[1] Buchanan Gray, op. cit. p. 374.
[2] Jochanan-ben-Zaccai, quoted in Headlam, *Life and Teaching of Jesus Christ*, p. 113.

have been excavated show the remarkable extent of Gentile influence on the sacred art of the period. They are of basilica type, divided into a nave and two side aisles by rows of columns supporting a balcony on three sides. But what is more significant is that in some of them are found representations in mosaic of the signs of the Zodiac and other emblems. Mr. W. G. Tachau, writing in the *American Jewish Year-Book* (vol. xxviii.), says that 'it can readily be seen that most of the Talmudic laws are violated in these Galilean buildings. . . . There is no doubt that human and animal figures were introduced in the decoration. . . . The remains of the decorative motives prove them to be Greco-Roman, and they show startling resemblances to the Byzantine character of ornament as exhibited in Constantinople and even central France.' The existing remains belong to a period slightly later than that with which we are dealing, but 'undoubtedly this theory which formulates the belief of a Greek origin, could be applied to synagogues of a much earlier date, but it is logical to suppose that these buildings of Galilee, which show such decided resemblance to the neighbouring Roman edifices, were copies from them, or at least were inspired by Roman influence.' There is then no doubt about the influence of Hellenistic art upon Galilee. But the same is true of semi-religious thought. Mr. Herbert Loewe has pointed out [1] that Galilee was the centre in which outside influence in the sphere of demonology was most strongly felt. 'It will almost invariably be found

[1] Hastings, *E.R.E.*, art. 'Demons and Spirits.'

74   SACRAMENTALISM

that Galilean teachers accepted while Judean teachers rejected, the existence of spirits. The numerous instances which the New Testament furnishes would have been impossible save in Galilee : there is a strong similarity between these and those adduced by Galilean Rabbis.' Nearly all the angelology and demonology in the Talmud occurs in the sayings of Galilean Rabbis. The main cause of the infiltration of these ideas, which were largely limited to Galilee—Judea on the whole being free from them—is found in the ' ever-growing intercourse with the Greek and Roman world, produced by commercial and political circumstances.'

Even Dr. Headlam, who thinks that on the whole foreign influences did not penetrate very deep, shows how different was the religion of the Sadducees, Scribes, and Pharisees from that of these northern people. ' Their religion was not the religion of Galilee.' Hellenism on the other hand had its witnesses on every side. ' Galilee was surrounded by Greek cities. . . . The columns and the pediments of Greek temples must have been visible from many a hill-top. The customs of the Gentiles must have been a matter of knowledge and observation in a manner not possible in the villages of Judea. While the holy city was remote from the direct traffic of the world, it flowed through Galilee. Ptolemais, Caesarea, Sebaste, Scythopolis, Gadara, Paneas, were all near.' It can scarcely be doubted that in such circumstances sacramental ideas would find an easy entry upon the soil of Galilee. We should not go as far as the Italian scholar, Macchioro,

THE BACKGROUND OF CHRISTIANITY 75

in thinking that Palestinian Judaism was riddled with Orphism, but we think that his French critic, Boulanger,[1] goes too far in ruling out all possible Orphic influence from the Holy Land. One may refuse absolutely to accept the religious tenets and customs of a neighbour and yet be influenced by the subtle atmosphere that pervades all his thinking. If one has already a natural affinity with his mode of thought it is obvious that such influence is all the more likely to occur. This is what we believe happened in several Jewish circles at this time.

One section of the unofficial Judaism in which foreign influences were particularly fruitful was that which produced the Apocalypses. It is disputed whether Hellenistic or Persian influence is the one in question here, but scholars are generally agreed that the Apocalyptists were unofficial laymen who were closely affected by the one or the other. In this connexion it is interesting to notice that it has been suggested, though without evidence, that the actual home of Apocalyptic was in Galilee.

Another and wider section that would be specially open to outside influences was that class which Professor Sanday long ago called 'the special seed-plot of Christianity,' the 'Am-Ha'arez or People of the Land. This title is applied in the Old Testament to the mass of the nation as distinct from the nobility, and in the New to those who 'knew not the Law' and were consequently regarded as accurst by the Pharisees. Whether or no this class was the most sincerely religious in the community is not clear;

[1] *Orphée*, ch. iii.

it is certain that it included 'publicans and sinners,' and that it formed the more immediate environment of our Lord and His disciples. And it is worthy of note that some at least of the Rabbis identified these People of the Land with the Galileans. It was among these folk that there was cherished the ideal of a Messiah who should come ' to be a light to lighten the Gentiles ' as well as to be the glory of God's people Israel. Possessed by this universalist spirit they would naturally have more sympathy with foreigners than was displayed by the rest of their countrymen, and would be particularly open to the infiltration of Gentile religious thought with all the sacramental implications that we have recently discussed.

But it is in a third group, that of the Essenes, that we have the clearest evidence of the infiltration of sacramental ideas. Of their cult Oesterley[1] has actually gone so far as to say that 'in some respects it was a mystery-religion.' Thus, although they eschewed animal sacrifices and anointing with oil, they had baptismal lustrations that were apparently sacramental, and the sacramental character of their solemn meals is sufficiently suggested by the obligation of the preparatory bath, the white robes and the blessing of the food.

It is among such unofficial circles that the precursors of the Christian sacraments must be sought. This judgment becomes especially probable if we are right in our conclusion that these circles were particularly open to such vague suggestions of hidden powers lurking within physical factors as would

[1] *Books of the Apocrypha*, p. 45.

emanate from the foreign cults. The severest opposition to the mysteries such as that manifested by the writer of Wisdom (xiv. 23) would be powerless to prevent such suggestions from bearing fruit, especially among a people whose worship was ultimately rooted in sacramental ideas. Perhaps it was this kind of feeling that before long made even certain orthodox Rabbis contend that baptism without circumcision was enough for proselytes. Baptism as an initiatory rite was thus already acquiring the implication of a change of status, of a new relation to God, and a still more definitely sacramental significance would be hard to escape when it was used so conspicuously by John. Similarly an oil sacrament is alluded to in the Book of Enoch.[1] This passage narrates how the Archangel Michael anoints Enoch with a perfumed and shining oil, which so changes his nature that he becomes like one of God's 'glorious ones' and never again needs earthly food. This was written in the period 1–50 A.D., and during the same half-century anointing for the purpose of healing evidently became so common as to need a merely casual mention from James (v. 14). Similarly in 4 Esdras (xiv. 39) there is mention of a drink, the colour of which is like fire and the effect such as to make wisdom grow in the breast and the heart utter understanding.[2] It is possible that something of the same atmosphere hovered about the sacred meals that had sprung up on Jewish soil, and although not strictly sacraments, might easily form the environment for such.

[1] Enoch xxii. 8 ; lvi. 2.   [2] Cf. 2 Enoch xxii. 8.

By the opening of the Christian era religious meals had become the vogue. Among the Jews it was now the custom to usher in every Sabbath with a common meal on the Friday evening. This Kiddush, as it was called, was held in the bosom of one's family, though later it might be held in the synagogue, but always there was bread and wine and a solemn blessing pronounced over them in the words of Gen. i. 31 to ii. 3, to which was added in the case of the wine, ' Blessed art Thou, O Lord our God, King of the universe, who createst the fruit of the vine,' and in the case of the bread, ' Blessed art Thou, O Lord our God, King of the universe, who bringest forth bread from the earth.'[1]

It is more than possible that this was the meal that our Lord was sharing with His disciples on the occasion of the 'Last Supper.' It is only the Synoptists who seem to identify that banquet with the Passover. The Fourth Gospel says very definitely that Jesus was crucified at the time of the slaying of the Paschal victim, that is, on the day of Preparation, the day before the Passover. As the Jewish day was reckoned from 6 p.m. to 6 p.m. and not, according to our fashion, from midnight to midnight, the Last Supper was also held, by this reckoning, on the day before the Passover. At first sight this would seem to destroy the Passover associations that have always clung about the Last Supper. But it may be doubted whether there is any real discrepancy. It has been suggested that just as

[1] Oesterley and Box, *Rabbinical and Medieval Judaism*, p. 188.

THE BACKGROUND OF CHRISTIANITY 79

the Jews had begun to usher in the Sabbath with a Kiddush, so they may have hedged about the Passover already, as they certainly did in a later day, with a similar meal, and the suggestion is especially credible in this case, as the Passover coincided with a Sabbath. It is likely that the Synoptists are using popular language in claiming the preparatory meal on the 'eve' as part of the festival, for the Passover Kiddush would naturally be coloured with all the thoughts appropriate to that commemoration.

But this does not exhaust the possibilities. Dr. Schweitzer, in a brilliant guess repeated by Dr. N. P. Williams,[1] has suggested another sort of common meal as the origin of the Eucharist. It is well known how often in Hebrew writings the future Messianic kingdom is pictured under the image of a Banquet. 'In this mountain,' says Isaiah (xxv. 6), 'shall the Lord of hosts make unto all peoples a feast of fat things.' In this feast Leviathan himself shall form the staple dish.[2] Our Lord said that many foreigners should there sit down with Abraham, Isaac, and Jacob,[3] while He Himself and His disciples would there pick up again the broken thread of their common meals.[4] The guess is that Jesus while on earth was accustomed to celebrate from time to time a ceremonial repast with His disciples in anticipation of this Messianic banquet.

If there is anything at all in this suggestion it would seem much more likely that, rather than institute some special meal for the purpose, Jesus would give

[1] In *Essays Catholic and Critical*, p. 403. [2] 4 Esdras vi. 52.
[3] Matt. viii. 11. [4] Luke xxii. 16.

this particular significance to the Kiddush which they were already accustomed to share in common. One learns from the Fourth Gospel how naturally He would use such an occasion as an opportunity for explanatory discourse, and the Messianic Kingdom might easily form the subject of many such talks.

These, then, are some illustrations of the richness and fertility of the soil in which Christian sacramentalism took root. The hard, dry literalism of the Pharisees is in strong contrast to the wealth of fancy and meaning that popular religion gave to common actions in other circles. Where so much was vaguely sacramental it is perhaps hardly necessary to ask whether there was any rite that one could call definitely a sacrament. At least oil and water could effect more than physical changes, a common meal had a sacred character, and the familiar words of the Kiddush conveyed a solemn blessing.

Let us add to this a reminder that we are dealing with the most syncretistic age in all history. Not far away, at Alexandria, Philo, a Jewish contemporary of Jesus, was busy combining Judaism, Platonism, Pythagoreanism, and Stoicism into one great system in which hard facts never fail to enshrine religious truth. Essenism has already shown its interesting 'example of elasticity within the pale of Judaism.' Before long the Fourth Gospel, the most definitely sacramentalist document in the Bible, will be written by an Aramaic-speaking Jew steeped in Hellenistic thought, while S. James, the

THE BACKGROUND OF CHRISTIANITY 81

most Judaistic of Christian letter-writers, will borrow a phrase ' the wheel of generation '[1] from the Orphic cult. And all around are the Greek cities with their flourishing mystery cults. Does it not become likely that Pharisaism did not after all set the tone in religion, but that the atmosphere in Palestine generally, and especially in that circle which was the seed-plot of Christianity, was much more sacramental than our knowledge of official Judaism would lead us to expect ?

In such an atmosphere the complete significance of a rite would certainly be compounded of more meanings than one. Here at least ' both . . . and ' is likely to come nearer the truth than ' either . . . or.' The baptism of John was both from heaven and of men ; it combined the Essene lustration and the proselyte initiation and added the profound moralism of the inspired prophet. The Last Supper was Kiddush, Messianic Banquet, Passover, and Covenant sacrifice all in one. Essentially Jewish as both undoubtedly were, they took their rise in an environment permeated with the spiritualism of the current Hellenistic teaching. ' No one,' as Bertholet has truly remarked, ' can understand the religion of the Jews . . . without a full intelligence of their astonishing faculty of assimilation.'[2]

[1] See Ropes on *S. James* iii. 6 ('Internat. Crit. Com.').
[2] Oesterley, *Books of the Apocrypha*, p. 58.

CHAPTER VII

THE TEACHING OF JESUS

WE have now come to the point where we must try to determine what is our Lord's own position in the history of sacramentalism. For modern students that raises a difficult question—how difficult can be seen at once if we compare the judgment of Dr. Schweitzer [1] on the one hand that, according to the Fourth Gospel, Jesus came into the world for the express purpose of inaugurating the era of effectual sacraments, with the guarded suggestion of Dr. Glover [2] on the other, that Jesus instituted no sacrament. Between Dr. Glover and the Fourth Gospel as thus interpreted there is as wide a gulf as it is possible to imagine.

The value of our own preliminary studies should here become apparent, for they help to determine for us the kind of intellectual and religious atmosphere in which Jesus and His immediate disciples lived. The mistake is too often made of trying to interpret sayings of Christ as if they were uttered *in vacuo*, or, still worse, of interpreting them only in the light of subsequent practice. We have to determine what construction He and His contemporaries would

[1] *Paul and his Interpreters*, pp. 202-3.
[2] *Conflict of Religions*, p. 158.

THE TEACHING OF JESUS

naturally put upon certain actions, what meaning certain words would naturally bear to Him who uttered them and to those who heard them. And that cannot be done without remembering the conceptual environment in which they were employed.

The evidence so far adduced serves to show that this environment was such as to make it natural to think in terms of sacraments. Men still loved and reverenced the Hebrew scriptures, and those scriptures taught that the physical universe was the creation of a good and bountiful God. There was thus no sharp antagonism between spirit and matter, and the Old Testament itself provided many examples of the conveyance of spiritual power by physical means. This sacramentalist attitude had been encouraged by the Hellenistic syncretism which had manifested itself most completely on the Pagan side in the Mysteries.

That Jesus shared this attitude it would be difficult to deny. For Him life was all of one piece: the heavens still declared the glory of God, as they did for the Psalmist, and the royal robes of the red anemones were tokens of the Father's care. Matter is the vehicle and instrument of spirit, and all three modes of sacramentalism, by object, action, and word, are employed by Him as instruments of His healing power. Clay becomes a salve, contact conveys virtue, and the use of His name expels demons.[1]

It looks, then, as if Jesus accepted simply and naturally the sacramentalist attitude of His day.

[1] Luke x. 17.

84 SACRAMENTALISM

Is there nothing more to be said than that ? In another connexion we are told that what struck people about His teaching was that He spoke with authority. It is instructive to trace this self-emanating authority in His sacramentalism also. The power conveyed by physical means is His own. Other men may pray to God for healing : He bestows it Himself. And this is possible because He identifies Himself so closely with His Father that all the hidden power of the universe is available to Him.[1] As the rays of the sun are focussed in a burning-glass, so unseen forces are concentrated through Him upon some desired point. And it is entirely characteristic that to Him the unseen is more important than the seen, the spiritual more real than the material. Indeed, if the Fourth Gospel is to be trusted, He habitually regarded the material universe as a faint shadow of the real world of spirit, identifying Himself whole-heartedly with the unseen reality. Thus He describes Himself as the real vine, the real door, the real light of the world. The sun that swings in the heavens and the other material existences are but pale reflexions of the intense reality that is in Him.

Looking back from the vantage-ground of a later day and a developed Christology we can see clearly enough the reasons that justify this claim. We see in Jesus of Nazareth God incarnate, Absolute Spirit expressing itself in space and time, using the human nature of Mary's Son as the instrument of redemption. As such Jesus is seen to be Himself ' the supreme

[1] John v. 19 ff. ; cf. Matt. xi. 27 (xxviii. 18).

sacrament, apart from which no other has use or meaning.[1] At present, however, we are trying to look at the matter not from the point of view of a later day but from that of a contemporary. But the effect is broadly the same. Jesus at least had 'seen the Father,' to be in fellowship with Him was to see the Father also, and it was the sacramental means employed by Him that inaugurated and cemented that fellowship.

Here, then, is a unique and stupendous development of sacramental thought. The Pagan world and Jesus' own ancestors of Hebrew race had begun with the material and groped their way to the spiritual, but He began with the spiritual and stooped to the use of the material. They, through blood and fat and incense, had offered spiritual gifts to God, but He, through means no less material, brought spiritual gifts from God to men. The method is the same, the orientation is different. It is from this vantage-point that we can best survey those two great sacraments that Christian tradition has most closely associated with Him—Baptism and the Supper of the Lord.

I

That Jesus looked upon His last meal with His disciples as an event of the greatest importance is evident from the intense longing implied in His words, ' With desire have I desired to eat this Passover with you before I suffer. . . . I will no more drink of the fruit of the vine till I drink it new with

[1] Quick, *Christian Sacraments*, p. 54.

you in My Father's kingdom.'[1] It is held possible that He looked upon it as the consummation of a series of Messianic banquets that was to be renewed in a fresh series after the inauguration of the Kingdom. But that this did not exhaust the significance of the last meal is evident from the solemnity of that culminating moment when He took bread and gave thanks and broke it and said, 'This is My Body.' The words would inevitably conjure up the thought of the Passover ; the bodies of Passover victims were to be eaten at this time, here was *His* Body. But the fact that the phrase is used in respect of bread and not of some slaughtered animal would emphasize the strangeness of the association, and would throw into strong relief the identification with His Body while allowing the thought of the Passover to fall into the background. It would make a merely metaphorical interpretation less easy, and would have a more sacramental sound to minds already attuned in some measure to that type of thought. Further, seeing the Bread broken and distributed in circumstances of the greatest solemnity, and experiencing the physical sensations of eating, they would have impressed upon them in the most vivid manner possible the feeling of an inward participation.

But what was that in which they participated ? He Himself had called it His Body. But certainly that did not mean the physical body of flesh and blood which stood there whole and intact before them. But what, after all, is the body ? Is it not simply the vehicle and instrument of the personality ?

[1] Luke xxii. 15 ; Matt. xxvi. 29 ; Mark xiv. 25.

And when the Lord said, 'This is My Body,' would not all the inherited tradition of the centuries as well as the diffused sacramentalism of their day combine to make the disciples feel that under the outward and visible envelope of the bread which He designated His Body He was conveying to them the gift of His personality?

Any doubt they may have felt about this must have been removed by the accompanying association of the wine with His Blood. For to the Jews, as we have seen, the blood meant one thing and one thing only, the life, or vital principle, of the victim. As such it was felt to be so sacrosanct that it could never be tasted by the worshipper but must always be returned to the God who gave it. Amid all the surprising events of this night none could have been more astounding to the disciples than that they should be thus suddenly ordered to break the inviolable tradition of the ages. They were to drink His Blood, and that could only mean that they were to take His life within themselves. That which they had so long in every sacrifice offered to God was now being conferred upon them. A vital principle was entering into them as they drank the cup, the life of their Master. So was reinforced the sense of personal union with Him that came to them as they ate His Body. It was the whole living Person in whom they were privileged to share, not the body only of some dead victim, but the personality of One who, in giving Himself, was instinct with life and power.

It is no part of our present task to discuss whether Jesus intended this scene to be reproduced in future gatherings of His disciples. That He once used the words Body and Blood in reference to the bread and wine is certain, and we have tried by careful historical inquiry to enter into the spirit of the time and understand what they meant to Him and to those who heard them. But the fact that His followers have actually attached the greatest importance to the repetition of the Last Supper has led to the question whether it can have had the same sacramental significance in the first instance as it has been held to have on subsequent occasions. Some scholars who hold to the highest sacramental interpretation of all subsequent Eucharists feel that this is not possible on the occasion when the Lord stood in His physical presence before His disciples. After He had ascended it was possible for Him to bestow an etherealized Body and Blood through the bread and wine, but while He was still ' in the flesh ' this could not be. And so it is suggested that the Last Supper was only a Eucharist by anticipation, a 'shadow Eucharist,' of which the substance was still to come.[1]

But if the interpretation given above is even approximately correct it is easy to see that we are not tied up to any such conclusion. The essential gift was the same all through. The ancients did not think of the personality as being indissolubly tied to the physical body even during the earthly life. The spirit might pass beyond the bounds of the flesh in dreams and thought, and there would be little difficulty in the suggestion that a living person could

[1] *Essays Catholic and Critical*, pp. 406, 423. Goudge, *I Corinthians*, pp. 105, 106.

THE TEACHING OF JESUS

communicate to others a share in his personality. And that, as we have seen, is the way in which Jesus thought of Himself as giving His Body and Blood, that is to say, a share in His complete, dynamic personality. No doubt after His ascension it was natural to think of this personality as clothed in the risen, etherealized body that He wore in the heavenly places. But the essential gift remained the same: it was only, so to speak, the clothing that differed.

We have here reached a position of commanding importance. As we shall see in a later chapter, the first generation of Christians found the supreme value of their Eucharist to lie in its substantial identity with the Last Supper. That identity cannot well be explained on any other ground than that taken up here. But that the ground is well chosen is confirmed by an interesting development in later sacramental theology. When in the doctrine of ' concomitance' (*Communicatio Idiomatum*, as applied to the Eucharist) the Church began to teach that he who received only one of the consecrated species received the whole gift, it is evident that she regarded that gift as whole and undivided, and identified it with the complete personality of the Lord.

2

When we come to consider the question of baptism we find ourselves faced by difficulties as grave as those we have encountered in the case of the Lord's Supper. Since doubts have been expressed both about the Fourth Gospel and the last verse of the

SACRAMENTALISM

First Gospel we have been deprived of the usual proof texts, and we have to meet the contention that baptism formed no part of the preaching and practice of Jesus. Our best plan will be to recount the order of events and to elicit their interpretation as we proceed.

In ancient religions ceremonial washings capable of a spiritual meaning were universal. In our Lord's own day His countrymen used them both in the Levitical ritual and for proselytes.[1] But in this time Baptism had been specially appropriated as the distinctive feature of the reforming movement inaugurated by John the Baptist. For his followers it involved a complete surrender of old vicious habits and the beginning of a new life of strict morality. There was therefore considerable consternation when the saintly Jesus of Nazareth presented Himself as one who wished to share in the ceremony. How could it be necessary or right for such an one ? No doubt He desired to associate Himself with all that was best in the contemporary religion, and He insisted that it was expedient so to ' fulfil all righteousness.' What in the result it actually meant for Him stands out quite clearly from the narrative : it meant a quickened sense of His Messianic sonship and of possession by the Spirit. From that moment He determined the lines upon which His tragic but saving mission was to be carried out. The Synoptists are agreed about the unique importance of this episode in the life of Christ.

[1] Moore, *Judaism*, i. 332 ff. Gavin, *Jewish Antecedents of the Christian Sacraments*, pp. 30 ff.

THE TEACHING OF JESUS

But subsequent events are not so clear. It looks as if, for a time at least, after John's imprisonment Jesus and His disciples carried on the work that the Baptist had laid down, although, in pursuance of His usual plan during the early part of His ministry of emphasizing His message rather than Himself, the Lord left the actual task of baptizing to His disciples. Presumably it became customary so to initiate all believers into the Kingdom. For them no doubt the ceremony would have all the significance that it possessed for the disciples of John, with some additional colouring from the known experience of Jesus at His own baptism.

Dr. A. Plummer suggests [1] that Jesus Himself continued the *preaching* work of John, while He had left His disciples to continue John's work in baptizing.[2] It is possible that they began even now to baptize in the name of Jesus. In any case it seems clear that whatever was done was carried out with the co-operation of Jesus, and was intended as a preparation for a baptism in which His followers should be made both sons of God and possessors of His Spirit. John indeed had promised that Jesus would baptize them with the Holy Spirit,[3] but the Fourth Gospel [4] and Acts [5] agree that this gift was not given in its fulness until Jesus was glorified. Yet on the very day of Pentecost it is with Baptism that Peter associates the reception of the Spirit.[6] It is probable, therefore, that those who had been baptized during

---

[1] *H.D.B.* i. 241.
[2] Mark i. 14, 15.
[3] Matt. iii. 11.
[4] John iii. 5 ; vii. 39.
[5] Acts i. 5.
[6] Acts ii. 38.

the intervening period received a promise of the Spirit which was fulfilled at Pentecost, and that from that moment all who were henceforth baptized were held to be qualified to share in the gift which those already baptized had received on that day.

The question how far all this was sacramental is not easy to settle. It is usual to contend that Baptism was not recognized as a sacrament till after Pentecost, but even Bousset admits that John's title of Baptist implies that he gave a deeper significance to the rite than others had done. As it was accompanied by repentance and remission of sins it could hardly escape acquiring at least a vaguely sacramental character; it altered a person's relation to God. Beyond that it is perhaps impossible for us to go. But such significance would be deepened after the striking events of the Lord's baptism, and would reach its culmination when the Spirit was fully given.

We conclude, then, that Jesus was in sympathy with the diffused sacramentalism of His day, that He accepted it, incorporated it into His own religion, and used it as a means of attaching His followers to Himself. No more than the Hebrew prophets did He distinguish between a 'spiritual' and a 'sacramental' religion, but equally with them He did distinguish between a moral and a non-moral interpretation of institutional religion. ' Go ye and learn what that meaneth, I will have mercy, and not sacrifice.'

It has sometimes been urged, even by those who see a certain element of sacramentalism in His teaching, that it is of the lightest kind—that, to follow the classification already adopted, if it is possible to find in His practice some association of spiritual power with words and actions, there is no such association of spiritual power with material objects. But this will not satisfy the evidence. It is true that in Baptism the emphasis is rather on the action of washing than on the water used. But in the Last Supper the emphasis was certainly not upon the breaking nor upon the eating, but most definitely and precisely upon the substances of bread and wine, or rather upon His Body and Blood. However we explain it we must then admit a sacramentalism of the third mode also.

The sacramentalism of Jesus was in its structure one with that of all the ages; it used the same methods, employed the same forms. But it differed from all other sacramentalism in its content. Grace and truth came by Jesus Christ. The sacraments as bequeathed by Jesus brought people into fellowship with Himself, with the Father, with the Holy Spirit, not with pagan Baalim nor even with Yahweh as imaged in the Law and the prophets. And a whole world of difference lies between the two. As so often happens in tracing an evolutionary process, we find that each phase, while rising naturally and almost inevitably from the stage before it, yet presents new and unanticipated features. The Christian sacraments represent the culmination of a searching process of evolution in which only the fittest could survive, and yet present themselves to the world as a new thing because of their association with the new creation in the incarnate Son of God.

CHAPTER VIII

THE APOSTOLIC CHURCH

THERE seems, then, enough evidence to justify us in believing that original Christianity shared that atmosphere of sacramentalism which pervaded the time and place of its birth. This conclusion is bound to affect our attitude towards the subject of the present chapter. That there was development in the sacramentalism of the Apostolic Church we shall see no reason to doubt ; indeed, we hope to show three stages of it as represented in the Acts, in S. Paul, and in the Fourth Gospel. But that there was any violent or revolutionary change we find it difficult to believe.

A current view is that Paul, and not Jesus, is the true author of institutional Christianity, and that the ' least of the apostles ' effected the great change by introducing sacramental elements derived ultimately from the mystery cults into the purely ethical, non-sacramental religion of Jesus. It is suggested that a type of Christianity quite different in this respect from the religion of the Pauline Gentile communities would be found among the Jewish Christians. But, as Kirsopp Lake admits, we know too little of the Judaistic Christians to hazard more

THE APOSTOLIC CHURCH 95

than a guess,[1] and the readiness of S. James to accept a sacrament of unction and to use Orphic terminology makes the guess particularly hazardous. Further, it must be remembered that none of the New Testament writers shows any knowledge of such a sacramentalist adulteration on the part of S. Paul. It is true that this argument is met by saying that Pauline influence had already affected the Synoptic writers so far, for instance, as to make them alter the date of the Last Supper. But if, as we have tried to show, the Synoptists are, roughly speaking, justified in their use of popular language, then the fact that even the primitive Jewish Christian community never makes any accusation against S. Paul of bringing about a revolutionary change in a sacramentalist direction must be allowed to close the question.

A. Baptism

1. Acts. In the primitive church of Jerusalem we find at least three sacramental rites: baptism, laying-on of hands, and breaking of bread. The first two fall together as complementary to each other, and Dr. Williams is certainly right in saying [2] that together with the preliminary act of confession they formed one great rite of initiation. But for the moment we shall concentrate our attention on the baptism proper. In one respect this continued and defined more clearly the significance of John's baptism; it actually brought about the remission

[1] *Earlier Epistles of S. Paul*, p. 390.
[2] *Essays Catholic and Critical*, pp. 374-7.

of sins.[1] But in two other respects it differed from John's baptism; it was 'in the name of Jesus' and it was 'with the Holy Spirit.' Both points are of very great importance.

To take the latter first. It has been suggested[2] that to 'baptize' is a metaphorical phrase not necessarily involving the use of water, and that the baptism with the Holy Spirit foretold by John and the risen Jesus,[3] and fulfilled at Pentecost and on other occasions was not, as a matter of fact, associated with water-baptism. Now there is no doubt that material for such a metaphor lay ready to hand,[4] and it is more than likely that no incident recorded in Acts definitely couples the gift of the Spirit with baptism. The one[5] incident that seems to do so[6] is best explained as a promise that they who were baptized into the Spirit-filled body would ultimately receive the gift of the Spirit too. And it is certainly true that the gift of the Spirit is generally coupled in Acts with the laying-on of hands. But there is one conclusion that we should be justified in drawing from the evidence: the gift of the Spirit is never entirely dissociated from baptism. It is most

[1] Acts ii. 38; xxii. 16.
[2] E.g. by Bezzant, *Modern Churchman* (October 1926), p. 339.
[3] Matt. iii. 11; Acts i. 5.
[4] Cf. Ezek. xxxvi. 25-27; xxxix. 29; and other literature cited by Abrahams, *Studies in Pharisaism and the Gospels*, i. 43.
[5] There is also a direct assertion of it in the Western text of Acts viii. 39.
[6] Acts ii. 38.

THE APOSTOLIC CHURCH

probable that those Christians who received the gift on the day of Pentecost had themselves been baptized either with John's baptism or with the form of baptism used by the Apostles after his decease. It is true that on a later occasion S. Paul found John's baptism insufficient, and baptized in the name of Jesus those who had received it. But that incident is mentioned by S. Luke in accordance with his characteristic method, because it marked a new departure. Such baptism in the name of Jesus preceded by a shorter or longer period the reception of the Holy Spirit. Only one instance is there in which the position is reversed. When S. Peter converted the household of Cornelius he was amazed to find that they became at once participants in the gift of the Spirit. Thereupon he baptized them. Normally, then, water-baptism was preparatory to Spirit-baptism, and where by exception the Spirit was given without the application of water the outward ceremony was speedily supplied.

Equally interesting questions arise in connexion with the phrase ' in the name of Jesus.' It is now generally agreed that this represents an earlier formula than the threefold name. But its precise meaning is far from clear. At one extreme it is suggested that it is simply the Christian designation for the rite that is thus distinguished from that ' of John.' But this explanation takes no account of the very emphatic words ' in ' or ' into the name.' At the other extreme it is suggested that the Name was repeated as a spell over the water with the object of thus imparting the Spirit to the water, which then became potent enough to recreate the life of the person baptized. But 1, the Name was almost certainly repeated not over the water but over the person; 2, it is the act of washing that is emphasized, not the element of water, as, for example, in the baptism of Jesus, where the dove descends not on the water but upon the Baptized; and 3, the suggested explanation brings in the crudest type of pagan sacramentalism: there is nothing Jewish about it. An intermediate explanation is possible. We have seen before how a name could be regarded as summing up a personality. An interesting extension of such use is seen in a late Talmudic phrase quoted by Abrahams, in which the baptism of a slave on his admission into the rank of freemen is described as 'baptism into the name of freedom.' Where the name was really that of a person it might carry by analogy some suggestion of incorporation into him, and the phrase would thus lead up to the Pauline expression, 'baptism into Christ,' with the implied suggestion of 'grafting' into Him.

2. S. Paul. When we come to the great apostle of the Gentiles it is important to remember the environment in which both he and his converts moved. The missionary churches were founded in the midst of that Hellenistic culture which had proved so rich a soil for the growth of the Mystery cults. That there was some sort of affinity between the churches and the cult societies is clear from what we know of the conditions of the church in Corinth and of the second-century schismatic leader Montanus,

THE APOSTOLIC CHURCH

S. Paul was always ready to become all things to all men if by any means he might save some, and the initiates of the cults were definitely among those who needed to be saved. But to the Christians the gods of the cults were evil demons, and the Church was the avowed enemy of the cults. It is most unlikely that the Church would consciously borrow from the cults, and a careful examination of the available evidence shows that such borrowing cannot be proved.[1] Yet it is incredible that the Christian society could live in close contact with another similar society and not be influenced. It is quite certain that Christian terminology, and the dates and customs of feasts were closely affected by such contact. But the influence goes further than that. Christian sacramentalism was able to express and explain itself and even to understand its own fundamental postulates more clearly than it could otherwise have done. Just as in later years the environment of the philosophic world enabled Christian theology to express itself in a form that has endured to our own day, so did Hellenistic sacramentalism enable the Church to draw out the implications of her original rites.

We have already seen that the object of the mysteries was to bring about a union between the believer and the Saviour God. It is remarkable that as we look through the passages in which S. Paul speaks of baptism we find just this union described as its result. Baptism is still ' in the name of the Lord Jesus Christ and in the Spirit of our

[1] Williams, *Essays Catholic and Critical*.

100 SACRAMENTALISM

God,'[1] but now for the first time the necessary inference is drawn that this means ' putting on Christ.'[2] In the Pauline doctrine that is the fundamental thing ; all else flows from that. But having put on Christ all the rest follows, dying with Him to sin and rising with Him to newness of life and abiding membership in His body.[3] Thus is sacramentalism raised to its sublimest heights.

But in one respect S. Paul's teaching differs *toto mundo* from that of the mysteries. His is no magical operation. All that is done is done by faith, and that implies a trust in the Divine which naturally issues in a spotless moral purity.[4] In S. Paul there is no more antithesis between faith and sacrament than there is between sacrament and morality.

3. The Fourth Gospel was written more than a generation after the Church's sacramental worship was well established, and it consequently has as its background the community of the faithful. The book is an attempt to make clear to baptized communicants the underlying truths of the Lord's person, life, and teaching. To do this effectively it is sometimes necessary to correct wrong impressions. Thus the author makes clear the true date of the Last Supper. He is very definite about the pre-existence of the Logos who was incarnate in Jesus. Yet he corrects the conclusion that Jesus is therefore a merely phantasmal appearance and affirms that He was a real flesh-and-blood incarnation of God. And it is evident that in the same way he is trying to

---

[1] 1 Cor. vi. 11.   [2] Gal. iii. 27.
[3] Rom. vi. 3 ; 1 Cor. xii. 12.   [4] Gal. iii. 26 ; Col. ii. 12.

correct false impressions about the sacraments. People have been too materialistic in their interpretation. He wishes to win them to more spiritual views while in no way seeming to belittle the importance of the outward rite. Therefore he omits the stories of the Lord's baptism and the institution of the Eucharist, which were in any case well known, and then finds room to draw out more fully than any other evangelist the Lord's teaching on these two subjects.

Perhaps it was his acquaintance with the ' mystery ' teaching of Asia Minor that enabled S. John to distinguish and emphasize so clearly the point that becomes his great contribution to the theology of Baptism. It is known that some of those who had submitted to the Taurobolium were said to have been ' born again ' or ' born again for ever.' In the Fourth Gospel we find our Lord teaching Nicodemus, ' except a man be born of water and the Spirit he cannot enter the kingdom of Heaven.' It is true that in the discourse the emphasis is on the Spirit rather than on the material element, but baptism is obviously understood as a well-known outward ceremony, and the evangelist is trying to bring out in the clearest possible way its inner significance. Here at least there is no suggestion that baptism with the Spirit is to be distinguished from water-baptism. In the faith and practice of the Church they had long been united : only people must not be allowed to forget what ' being born of the Spirit ' really meant.

We see, then, the steps by which the explanation of

baptism gradually attained completion and clarity in New Testament times. The Christian rite followed naturally upon that of John and had as its main significance the change from a life of sin to one of moral effort. In the earliest Christian community after the Ascension the leaders of the new brotherhood regarded it as the natural rite of admission into their circle, and began to distinguish sharply between the baptism of John and baptism into the name of Jesus, associating the latter clearly with the remission of sins and less clearly with the gift of the Spirit. S. Paul saw it as the inevitable concomitant of faith in Jesus, accomplishing in the believer a personal union with his Lord. And S. John, having these conceptions in mind, brings out as the fundamental explanation and justification of them all the fact that baptism involves a new birth from above, by which the believer is introduced into a fresh spiritual life, just as by his physical birth he had been introduced into life on the natural plane.

B. *The Lord's Supper*

The Lord's Supper follows much the same lines of development as Baptism. We can see the sacramental significance being worked out in successive stages. While it is certainly true, as we have seen, that such significance is present from the beginning, there can be little doubt that Hellenistic methods of thought help a good deal in its elucidation.

1. Acts. The first significant thing is that the Last Supper appears to have been regularly repro-

THE APOSTOLIC CHURCH 103

duced without any break, at least from the time when the Christian community leaped to a sense of entity and unity at Pentecost. It is disputed whether Jesus had actually commanded such continuance. For the best discussion of the point we must refer the reader to Professor Williams's exhaustive and decisive examination in *Essays Catholic and Critical*. We ourselves must be content with pointing out that while it is no doubt true to say that if the words ' Do this ' are an interpolation in S. Luke's Gospel, S. Paul remains the only authority for dominical command, yet the words are not in themselves of fundamental importance. Since men for whom obedience to the Lord's commands had become the very breath of life repeated this service unanimously and without apparent question, we may be very sure that such continuance was in line with His known wishes.

Were other argument needed, it would be supplied by that sacramental character which we saw to be inherent in the Last Supper. Of course, if ' the special Eucharistic features of the Last Supper were dramatic symbols for the benefit of those then present and needing light on the tragedy overhanging their faith,' [1] and nothing more—if, that is, they were just a piece of play-acting, then there would obviously be very little point in repeating them after the tragedy was over. But if the disciples felt that they had in some sense or other eaten the Lord's Body and drunk His Blood on that occasion, and if they had ever reflected that that might mean sharing in

[1] Bartlet and Carlyle, *Christianity in History*, p. 79.

SACRAMENTALISM

His undying life, then there would be every reason why they should ask if that could not be repeated.

The social side of the meal was emphasized. The family feeling that had animated Jesus and His disciples at their weekly Kiddush still bound together the little circle of believers. Perhaps it is this that gives to combined meal and service its characteristic name of 'breaking of bread.' But that name may also refer back to that solemn 'breaking' in the Upper Room, when Jesus took the bread and said, 'This is My Body.' There is no evidence during this period of any sacred community meal in which the repetition of this solemn action did not form a part.

2. If in Acts it is thus on union with one another that emphasis naturally lies, in S. Paul, while that side is not unnoticed, it is rather union with God that is stressed. In the working out of this element of the doctrine we find, as in the case of baptism, a marked similarity with the teaching of the mystery cults. S. Paul himself makes the comparison. It forms part of his argument against those who would eat meats that had been offered in sacrifice to idols. To do so, says S. Paul, would be to share in the nature of those idol-gods themselves, and those gods are devils. 'You cannot share at once in the Lord and in the demons.'[1] Remembering the environment in which S. Paul worked, one can have no doubt about the way in which this would be understood both by the Apostle and by his converts. Indeed, he makes the sense clear in the same passage. 'The cup of blessing which we bless, is it not a participation in

[1] 1 Cor. x. 16–21.

THE APOSTOLIC CHURCH 105

the Blood of Christ ? The bread which we break, is it not a participation in the Body of Christ ? ' And the sense is borne out by the judgment foretold against those who ' discern not the Lord's Body.'

But union with God is not the only point emphasized by S. Paul in his doctrine of the Supper. The meal is not merely a means of fellowship with God : it is also a ' memorial ' of Christ's death, and those who repeat it ' do show forth the Lord's death till He come.' [1] But this ' memorial ' is not a mere reminder. In view of all the sacrificial terms associated with the rite in S. Paul's references to it, and in view of its connexion with the Passover, there is a definite fragrance of sacrifice left clinging to the rite itself, though the precise implications of this are not brought out.

These, then, are the two things that the Lord's Supper means to S. Paul, union and memorial. It is remarkable that among those who have looked upon the great apostle to the Gentiles as the sinister innovator frustrating the simple intentions of the Founder of Christianity, there are some who see the vital change in the one particular and some in the other. The fashionable modern view has been that while Jesus held a simple social meal with His disciples and they continued it as a memorial of Him, S. Paul changed it into a rite of sacramental union with deity. Lietzmann,[2] on the other hand, has recently tried to show that while Jesus instituted a communion, Paul changed it into a sacrificial memorial.

[1] 1 Cor. xi. 20–26.
[2] *Messe und Herrmmahl*, pp. 250–5.

SACRAMENTALISM

Such interpretations go far towards cancelling each other out. When we turn to the records we look in vain for any knowledge of a momentous change wrought by S. Paul. The apostle himself is very emphatic in contending that all his teaching is in line with the best authority. ' I received of the Lord that which I also delivered unto you.' The Corinthians have many complaints against him, but none on the score that he is teaching a new Eucharist. The Jewish Christians oppose bitterly his innovations with regard to the Law, but they never appear to suspect for a moment that he is making innovations in the principal rite of Christian worship. Is it not then probable that just as the double form of the rite, breaking of bread and communion, is the same in both Acts and Epistles, so the doctrine is essentially the same too, though Paul seems to make explicit what was only implied in Acts?

3. The Fourth Gospel, as we have seen, does not repeat the account, already well known to its readers, of the institution of the Eucharist, but gives instead the great discourse on the Bread of Life in chapter vi. This is sometimes interpreted as if it were meant to apply only to a moral assimilation of the character of Christ. We need not deny this meaning so long as it does not exclude a primary reference to sacramental communion. In the days when this Gospel was written, the Eucharist was regularly celebrated, and a phrase about eating the flesh of Christ would have as necessary a sacramental implication as it would bear if it were uttered in an Anglican pulpit to-day.

THE APOSTOLIC CHURCH

S. John, says Sir Edwyn Hoskyns,[1] 'defines Christian worship as eating the flesh of the Son of Man and drinking His blood. He is acutely conscious that this language is capable of a purely materialistic interpretation. The Jews roundly declare it to be blasphemous anthropophagy, and all but the true disciples are shocked and leave the Church because of this language. But S. John refuses to ease the language. In repeating the saying he retains the word " flesh " and substitutes a more crudely material word meaning " munch " for the word " eat." He is therefore referring to a rite in which physical eating is integral, and he is not prepared to compromise the fact.'

The language used is, therefore, that of union—and of union most dramatically and intensely conceived—with the whole process of the incarnate life of the Son of God. In that process there are three distinct moments—the moment when the Word was made flesh, the moment when the Word-made-flesh was offered for the life of the world, and the resurrection. Participation in this process on the part of the believer is necessary for salvation, and participation is by means of the sacrament. 'Except ye eat the flesh of the Son of Man and drink His blood, ye have not life in yourselves. He that eateth My flesh and drinketh My blood hath eternal life, and I will raise him up at the last day.' The new thing here is the strong emphasis upon the guarantee of a personal resurrection for the believer. The similarity of this with the intention of the mystery cults to

[1] *Report of Anglo-Catholic Congress* (1927), p. 52.

guarantee immortality does not need to be pointed out. It may easily have been contact with the claims of these cults that brought out so strong a rival emphasis. But there is one momentous difference. In S. John it is no semi-magical act or formula that enables a man to escape the demons and find protection through his hero-god, but all is done by the loving, pervading, all-powerful Spirit who is at once the Spirit of Jesus and of the Father Himself.

. . . .

Such, then, is the way in which Eucharistic doctrine developed during the period covered by the New Testament. That there was development, no modern scholar would wish to deny. But does not that development bear all the marks of a true and justifiable continuity? Acts shows us the primitive Church repeating the distinguishing features of the Last Supper, and actually places S. Paul among those who participated in the repeated rite. S. Paul himself gives us the explanation that he attached to what he did, pointing out the twofold aspect of the sacrament as memorial and communion. S. John reiterates this with emphasis, adding only its corollary in the guaranteed resurrection of the believer. And he is so sure of this explanation that he can afford to neglect the familiar story of the institution and use his opportunity of showing how its significance was already adumbrated in the earlier teaching of the Saviour. We contend that this is as much as we can really know of the mind of Christ in this matter. Any attempt to get behind these records and to interpret Christ's intention afresh is bound to be subjective in the last degree ; of other certain warrant there is none.

For all to whom the New Testament stands as the authoritative norm of Christian life and worship this is in practice enough. We are given the facts of the sacraments and are assured in no uncertain terms of the benefits that issue from the devout reception of them. But that is not to say that there is no region left for further inquiry. How the sacraments act, and why, are questions not answered in the New Testament, and that is the field of speculation in which the best intellects of many generations occupied themselves not altogether in vain. The results of these successive efforts we must now proceed to summarize.

CHAPTER IX

THE ANTE-NICENE FATHERS

THE central fact in the piety of the Early Church was the clearness with which the believers perceived Christ's presence in their midst. He had appeared frequently between the resurrection and the ascension. Even after the latter event He had appeared to S. Stephen, S. Paul, and the seer of the Apocalypse. But whether seen or unseen He was always there. It seemed no presumption for the Council of Jerusalem to say that their own conclusions were those of His Spirit. S. Paul felt Him as the animating power of all his activities. Martyrs like Ignatius and Polycarp went to their death sustained, if not by the sight of Him who is invisible, at least by a firm faith in the real presence of their King who had saved them.[1]

But if this Presence was thus ever about them, it was mediated more especially in the solemn repetition of the sacramental portion of His last meal with His disciples. In this respect at least there is no distinction to be drawn between Lord's Supper, breaking of bread, and Eucharist. Gustav Truc [2] is

[1] Cf. Schlatter, *Geschichte der Ersten Christenheit*, pp. 4–8. Nock, *Essays on the Trinity and the Incarnation*, p. 47.
[2] *Les Sacraments*, p. 8.

certainly right in seeing in this mystic presence with His own the original and invariable background of the rite. Only we must be careful not to use the word 'mystical' as if it were somehow opposed to 'real.' The presence was mystical only because it was capable of perception by senses finer than those of the gross material frame. Hence the careful and exact repetition of the circumstances of the first institution was a 'memorial' in a fashion infinitely richer than that implied by memory or recollection or reminder. In reproducing the events of that memorable night it reproduced also the very presence of Him who had then bestowed upon His followers the gifts of His individuality and His vital power. And this was true whether the rite were performed at the table of some wealthy believer or at the monumental slab in the cubiculum of some catacomb or in a dark recess of some mine.

On the first occasion the Presence had been confined to the small family circle of the disciples. So now it was natural that it should be available only to those who had been admitted to the family circle by the rite of initiation, consisting of confession, baptism, and laying-on of hands. Between the close of the New Testament and the Council of Nicea there seems to have been no great development in the doctrine of this rite. It brought the forgiveness of sins, the birth of a new life, and made the participant one of that many-membered body through which the presence of the Christ made itself felt.

Baptism was thus intensely sacramental with a sacramentalism essentially of action. A spiritual change was effected in the condition of the believer by plunging him beneath the water or by pouring water on his head as he stood in a stream or tank. But there was also a word-sacrament in so far as stress began to be laid on the Name, whether of Jesus or of the Trinity, in which the candidate was baptized. And, further, some approach to a sacrament of object was beginning when a mysterious potency was ascribed to the holy water that was set aside for use in the ceremony.

But for those who had thus been made members of the Body of Christ His presence was regularly mediated to them by the great central service which combined in itself all three forms of sacrament. It is sometimes assumed that the Lord's Supper, in so far as it was a sacrament at all, was such only in virtue of the whole action of the rite. We need not, indeed, dispute the view that the mystical presence of the Master was felt throughout the service. But all the evidence goes to show that the Presence was especially associated with the bread and wine, and this was further enforced by the growing emphasis placed upon the words of institution or upon the invocation of the Holy Spirit recited over the two elements. Thus both actions and words served to emphasize the fact that it was the sacramentalism of object that was of primary importance here. In baptism that type of sacramentalism was late and secondary, but in the Eucharist it was original and all-important.

This is sometimes obscured by the common confusion between the Agape and the Eucharist, which sometimes goes even to the length of regarding the

Eucharist as an offshoot from the charity-feast. But it is more than doubtful whether there was ever any vital connexion between the two. Indeed, if we may accept the result of the elaborate investigation recently undertaken by Dr. Karl Völker,[1] the Agape first came in as a charity meal with a devotional setting during the second half of the second century in connexion with the struggle against the Gnostics. This theory successfully disentangles the Eucharist and sets it clear in its straight line of development from the original Last Supper.

But such development as took place was a development of explanatory method and not a development of essential idea. There was never, for instance, any period during which the bread and wine were regarded as merely ineffectual 'symbols.' In this matter the words of Dr. Harnack[2] are sufficient. 'What we nowadays understand by "symbol" is a thing which is not that which it represents; at that time "symbol" denoted a thing which, in some kind of way, really is what it signifies; but, on the other hand, according to the idiom of that period, the really heavenly element lay either in or behind the visible form without being identical with it. Accordingly the distinction of a symbolic and realistic conception of the Supper is altogether to be rejected.' *A fortiori* this excludes the view that grace was conveyed not through the symbols but on occasion of their use, as it also excludes the pleasant but fanciful theory

---

[1] *Mysterium und Agape*, pp. 198–202.

[2] *History of Dogma*, ii. 144–5; cf. *Mission and Expansion of Christianity*, i. 228–9.

114 **SACRAMENTALISM**

that there was some specifically Hebraic conception of sacraments as 'words for the senses' communicating 'truth embodied in a tale.'[1] The tendency to connect the realization of the Presence with the very nature of the symbol was there from the beginning, and was indeed justified by the words of the Founder.

We can find, then, no evidence of progress in Christian thought about the *fact* of the Real Presence. Assurance that the Lord was really there is of the essence of this sacrament from the beginning. But this is not to deny that there was considerable development in the manner of conceiving the *mode* of the Presence. During the period with which we are now dealing, many efforts were made to explain the mystery. It is possible to group these efforts into different schools of thought. We can distinguish three centres of development, two of them Eastern and the third Western.

I

The first is what one might call the Incarnational School of Asia. It may well derive from Ephesus, for it continues the Johannine tradition and seems to be based on the view that the bread and wine become the Body and Blood of Christ in such a way that they have the power to build up a new, invisible, and immortal body in the being of him who partakes of them. Thus the famous passage in the Fourth Gospel says, 'He that eateth My

[1] Bartlet and Carlyle, *Christianity in History*, p. 150.

THE ANTE-NICENE FATHERS 115

flesh and drinketh My blood hath eternal life, and I will raise him up at the last day.' Similarly to Ignatius (c. 110 A.D.) the Eucharist is the 'bread of God' which is the 'medicine of immortality,' the antidote that preserves us from death and ensures us 'life for ever in Jesus Christ.'[1] So also Justin Martyr (c. 150 A.D.), who was born in Palestine and knew Ephesus as well as Rome, says of the Eucharist : ' We do not receive it as common bread or common drink ; but just as Jesus Christ our Saviour, made flesh by the word of God, had both flesh and blood for our salvation, so also we have been taught that the food over which thanksgiving has been made by the prayer of the Word that is from Him—that food from which our blood and flesh are by assimilation nourished—is both the flesh and the blood of the Jesus who was made flesh.'[2]

It is clear that this view involves belief in a threefold process, first an incarnation of the Logos, by which God became flesh ; next an analogous process by which the bread and wine become the flesh and blood of the incarnate Jesus ; and lastly a process by which our own flesh and blood are impregnated and so made immortal by the sacramental flesh and blood of Christ. Irenaeus (c. 180 A.D.), who was a native of Asia Minor though afterwards resident in Gaul, pushes the same type of thought a stage farther back, and begins with the Spirit permeating all nature. ' As a cutting of the vine planted in the ground becomes fruit in its season, and as a grain of wheat falling into the ground and being decomposed

[1] Eph. v. 20.   *Ap.* i. 66.

116   SACRAMENTALISM

rises manifold by the operation of the Spirit of God, who contains all things, and then through the wisdom of God comes to the use of man and receiving the word of God becomes Eucharist, which is the body and blood of Christ ; so also our bodies being nourished by it and laid in the earth and decomposed there shall rise at the due season, the Word of God granting them resurrection to the glory of our God and Father.'[1] Or again, ' As the bread of the earth, receiving the invocation of God, is no longer common bread but Eucharist, made up of two things, an earthly and a heavenly, so also our bodies, partaking of the Eucharist, are no longer corruptible, having the hope of resurrection to eternity.'[2]

2

A second group of writers form what may be called in this connexion the Mystical School of Alexandria. They are intensely Platonic. To them the unseen world is more real than the seen, and material things are symbols or allegories of spiritual. This has led many commentators to interpret their language in a merely pictorial or representative sense. But that is to be guilty of an anachronism. Dr. Darwell Stone[3] has pointed out that the Alexandrines borrowed the term ' symbol ' from the Pagan mysteries, and that it was used by them in the same sense as at once the sign and vehicle of divine gifts. This is in complete agreement with the interpreta-

[1] *Adv. Haer.* v. ii. 3.   [2] *Ibid.* IV. xviii. 5.
[3] *Doctrine of the Holy Eucharist*, i. 30.

tion that we have already seen Dr. Harnack put upon the word.

Starting from this conception it is natural that Clement of Alexandria (head of the catechetical school, c. 190–203 A.D.) should emphasize the spiritual much more strongly than the physical. Thus he says,[1] 'the flesh and blood of the Lord is the apprehension of the divine power and essence.' Again, while he can aver that the Body is Faith and the Blood Hope, yet he also maintains [2] that the bread, when 'hallowed by the potency of the Name,' has been changed 'by potency into a spiritual potency,' and he likens the Lord feeding His children on His own flesh and blood to a mother feeding her infant from her own body.

In the same way Origen, a pupil of Clement and his successor as head of the catechetical school, uses language that shows no sense of incongruity between what might seem to a modern to be two extremes, sometimes explaining the flesh and blood of the Lord as if they were His words, and sometimes being so sure that they are verily His body as to argue from the care actually bestowed upon them to the care that we ought to give to His words. 'If for the protection of His body ye take so great care, and are right to take it, can ye suppose that to be careless of the word of God is a less offence than to be careless of His body?'[3]

What was the normal language of this school may perhaps be best judged from a letter of Dionysius of Alexandria. Writing in 257 to the Bishop of

[1] *Strom.* v. 40, 66.   [2] *Exempla*, 82.   [3] *In Ez. Hom.* xiii. 3.

118   SACRAMENTALISM

Rome about one who, having been baptized by heretics, was in grave doubt whether he ought to continue to receive communion without being rebaptized, he describes him as having 'for a long period heard the Thanksgiving and joined in saying the Amen and stood at the Table and stretched out his hand to receive the holy Food and received it and partaken of the body and blood of our Lord Jesus Christ.'[1]

In the teaching of the Alexandrines we thus seem to have instead of the 'incarnational' theory of the Asiatics a mystical replacement of the bread and wine by the spiritual body and blood of the Lord. The material elements do not disappear from the physical senses, but they are neglected by the perception of faith, which grasps the hidden Reality associated with them. This perception is in itself so satisfying that the method of the association is hardly made a subject of investigation.

3

The third group is what one may call the Legalist School of Carthage. A convenient point of transition is found for us, curiously enough, in the fiery ex-lawyer Tertullian (c. 200), who uses 'symbolic' language, saying that the Bread is a 'figure' of the Body and that it 'represents' the Body. But the caution already uttered in connexion with the word 'symbol' applies here too. The 'figure' by no means excludes the actual presence of that which is

[1] Eus. *H.E.* vii.

symbolized, while the word 'represent' is used frequently in the sense of actually exhibiting or making present what was invisible or absent before, and only rarely in the sense of bringing an idea to the mind. So in arguing against the Docetics Tertullian proves that our Lord's earthly body was real because it has its 'figure' in the Eucharist, just as you cannot have a shadow unless there is a material substance to cast it.

But what is especially interesting about Tertullian in this respect is his belief in the close connexion between the flesh and the soul. In the sacraments generally the soul is affected through the flesh, and in the Eucharist particularly it is the flesh that is first fed by the body and blood of Christ. 'The flesh is washed that the soul may be cleansed from stain; the flesh is anointed that the soul may be hallowed; the flesh is signed with the cross that the soul too may be guarded; the flesh is overshadowed by the imposition of hands that the soul too may be strengthened by the Spirit; the flesh feeds on the body and blood of Christ that the soul too may be made full of God. They are joined together in action, they cannot therefore be separated in reward.'[1] Even the petition, 'Give us this day our daily bread,' is made to include a request for the Lord's body, and Tertullian is equally anxious with Origen that no drop or crumb shall come to unworthy use.

There is thus a double significance in Tertullian's teaching. On the one hand there is an emphasis on the thing done in the physical sphere bringing its

[1] *De Res. Carn.* 8.

appropriate reward in the spiritual domain, which agrees well with his forensic attitude in the rest of his theology. On the other, there is a somewhat surprising readiness to see an intimate relation between the material and the spiritual which is quite in keeping with the sacramentalism that we have analysed in Eastern writers. The best-known example of this second tendency is to be found in his reference to the original waters of creation, which, he says, brought forth abundantly the moving creature that hath life as a warning that the waters of baptism would also have the power of producing life.[1]

Cyprian, who had also practised as an advocate, and was Bishop of Carthage from 248 to 258, carried on the teaching of his master in both respects. He narrates several stories of people who were prevented from making an unworthy communion by miracles that occurred in connexion with the sacred species, as, for instance, when one who had committed an act of apostasy found that the ' holy thing ' had become a cinder in his open hands.[2] This points to a considerable rigidity in the interpretation of the mode of the sacramental presence. But this precision is more marked in his development of the idea of the Eucharistic sacrifice. This offering is made by the priest in the place of Christ, and its efficacy consequently depends upon the precise imitation of the acts performed by Christ. Thus he defends the practice of mingling water with the wine on the ground that ' that priest truly performs his office in

[1] Gen. i. 20 ; *De Bapt.* iii.   [2] *De Laps.* 26.

THE ANTE-NICENE FATHERS 121

the place of Christ who imitates that which Christ did, and then offers in the Church to God the Father a real and complete sacrifice when he begins to offer as he sees Christ Himself offered.'[1]

What most clearly distinguishes these African fathers from their Eastern colleagues is their conception of grace as the instrument of salvation. To characteristic Western thought salvation was the escape of the sinner from a sinful world and from the doom that threatened it. Grace was the influence that gave the sinner strength for the rescue. As early as Tertullian we find grace thought of as a kind of power that is poured into a man from without. It was easy and natural then to think of the sacraments as the channels along which this divine power was conveyed, and it was even possible to think of the precise amounts of grace that might be procured by each recourse to any sacrament. But the characteristic Eastern method of thought was quite different. Here salvation was brought about by a certain divine alchemy which changed poor, weak humanity into something godlike. To the Asiatics and the Alexandrines the purpose of the sacraments was to build up in the believer a new man, to transform his sinful, mortal nature into something that was at least semi-divine and immortal. Thus the sacraments were the means by which the Incarnation might have its full effect in the life of the individual. This view of the scheme of redemption was put most succinctly and most daringly by Athanasius, ' God became man that we might become God.'[2] Logically, therefore, it was

[1] *Ep.* lxiii. 14.   [2] *De Inc.* liv. 3.

intensely important to believe that Christ, perfect God and perfect man, was completely given to the faithful in the Lord's Supper. This helps to explain the immense interest taken by the Easterns in all Christological questions. It was just because their feeding upon the Saviour in the Eucharist was so important for their own salvation that it was necessary to make sure that He upon whom they fed touched at all points both their own nature and God's. Otherwise they could have no guarantee that their own change from mortal to immortal would be assured.

Here, then, in the ante-Nicene period we have already the beginnings of that process of explanation that has continued ever since. But as yet it has not gone very far, and many of the difficulties that beset later thinkers have not yet been felt : the atmosphere is that of the New Testament rather than the Middle Ages. The quiet simplicity of Acts, with its calm assurance of the ever-abiding presence of Christ, has its counterpart in the mystical teaching of Alexandria ; S. Paul's reliance on exact tradition is more than paralleled by the Legalist School of Carthage ; S. John's emphasis upon the connexion between eternal life and the assimilation of the flesh and blood of the Saviour has its logical successor in the Incarnational School of Asia. It is the last of these (which was the first in time) that comes nearest to offering an explanation of sacramental method. How the divine Redeemer can be enshrined within the material elements, and how by the consumption of those material elements He can be communicated to the believer, are questions left for future ages to wrestle with. But the very analysis of the problem, even if only implied and not explicitly made, opened the way for attempts at explanation that became inevitable as the centuries passed. Before we enter upon those inevitable discussions we shall do well to notice the happy freedom from such anxieties that marked the first three centuries of our era. There is evidence of providential ordering in the fact that during all those years of persecution the Church was sustained by unswerving belief in the sacramental presence of her Lord. It was only after external peace had been won that men found leisure to evolve precise theories of the method of the sacramental presence. And when certain of those explanations became authoritative some of the old freedom was necessarily lost.

CHAPTER X

THE MIDDLE AGES

THE medieval period was, for our subject, a period of definition. Definition implies limitation, and we certainly become aware that we are passing out of a large room of free interpretation into a confined space of necessary exactitude. In some respects the hardly won precision made for clearness in understanding and for ease in practical use. By the end of the Middle Ages, however, the new thought generated by regained access to the writers of the earlier period found this precision a prison-house and endeavoured to break free from it in the upheaval of the Reformation. In this chapter we consider the process of definition at work in divers respects during the thousand years from A.D. 500 to 1500.

I

Already in the fourth century belief in the Real Presence at the Eucharist had led to a concentration of thought upon the outward means by which the Presence became available. This in itself was very characteristic of the western mind which could not follow the typical mysticism of the East in its grasp

THE MIDDLE AGES 125

of the spiritual at the cost of the material. Nevertheless it was in the East that the first notice of this development was given. Jerusalem as a centre of pilgrimage would be open to influences from all parts of Christendom, and the devotion of worshippers would be affected both by the association of the sacred places and by contact with so many devout believers from different parts of the world. It was therefore natural that an advance in the statement of eucharistic doctrine should take place there. The presence of the Lord so emphatically realized after the consecration seemed to imply of necessity some change in the elements themselves. They must have been 'converted' from their former natural condition into another which was supernatural.

The first writer to use the language of conversion in this sense was Cyril of Jerusalem (315-386). His words are quite unequivocal: 'The bread of the Eucharist after the invocation of the Holy Spirit is no longer simple bread but the body of Christ.'[1] 'Whatever the Holy Spirit has touched is surely consecrated and changed.'[2] In this Cyril is supported by the Gregory who was Bishop of Nyssa in Cappadocia from 372 to 395. This great defender of Nicene theology exhausts the resources of the Greek language to express his belief in a transformation of the bread and wine. 'Rightly do we believe that the bread which is consecrated by the Word of God is "transmade" into the body of God the Word.' . . . 'He "transelements" the nature of visible things into that immortal thing by virtue of

[1] *P.G.* xxi. 3. [2] *P.G.* xxiii. 7.

the consecration.'[1] Thus the East accepts, and makes its own, language that would have been more natural in the West. And this continues until John of Damascus, the last of the Fathers (c. 676–767), who compares the transformation of bread into flesh when eaten by man with the process by which bread is transformed into the flesh of Christ when consecrated in the Eucharist.[2] Here, then, we have the first definite advance in precision of statement. If the earlier period has witnessed the firm establishment of sacramentalism in the very centre of the Christian system, this is the first actual limitation of the method by which the sacramental process is believed to work.

2

A second point about which a more exact definition came to be made was that of the efficacy of the sacraments. In its beginning the discussion of this question is connected with the great name of S. Augustine of Hippo. He found himself on entering upon the work of his see in controversy with the Donatists, who had effected a schism on the ground that some Church leaders had behaved badly in the persecutions, and that therefore their ministrations were not such as could be profitably received. Against them Augustine maintained that within the Church any duly ordained minister, bad or good,

[1] *Catechetical Oration*, xxxvii.; cf. Srawley's trans. pp. 111, 112 with notes.
[2] The same thought is in Greg. Nyss. loc. cit.

could profitably administer the sacraments, while outside the Church no man could do so. What, then, was the difference between sacraments within and without the Church? It would not do to say that the latter were no sacraments, because he already held that Baptism and Ordination conferred an indelible character. He therefore drew an important distinction between validity and efficacy, between the sacrament and the virtue of the sacrament. There was a difference between possessing a thing and possessing it profitably. Only those could possess a sacrament profitably who presented no bar to its internal operation upon the soul. Therefore while valid sacraments might be found in schism, efficacious sacraments were only to be found in the Church, for 'they could not have the grace of God who did not love the unity of God.'

This opened up the more subtle question how this efficacy came about. The difference between the sacrament and the virtue of the sacrament was not the only distinction pointed out by the great African teacher. Within the sacrament itself he discerned two things. There was the outward sign and there was the thing signified. This double character was to S. Augustine the distinguishing note of the New Testament sacraments. He described the sacraments of the Old Testament as those which promised a Saviour, while those of the New Testament gave salvation. In the case, then, of these effective signs of the new law, what was the precise relation between the sign and the thing signified? And, more definitely, how is the latter made effective for the believer who approaches the sacrament with the right dispositions? These are questions which still receive various answers.

S. Augustine's own mind seems hardly to have been made up on the matter. Sometimes he uses language that might lead one to suppose that he viewed sacraments as mere outward indications of a grace that is given or as conditions of our receiving grace, and much post-Reformation thought has followed him in this. But generally, while he regards grace as wider than the sacraments, he speaks of them as divinely appointed channels through which grace necessarily flows. There was, however, a difficulty about this: it seemed to imply that material things could be the cause of spiritual effects. Subsequent thinkers puzzled a good deal over this difficulty. It is of course the objection that is often brought against sacramental teaching in our own day. But it is a mistake to think that it is altogether modern. It was felt with especial force in the thirteenth century, and the Seraphic Doctor, S. Bonaventure, taught that sacraments were only the occasions of grace, divinely appointed indeed, and guarantees without which one could not be sure of receiving grace, but still not themselves the immediate cause of grace.

S. Bonaventure's contemporary, the Angelic Doctor, S. Thomas Aquinas, sought to find another way out of the difficulty. It was possible to think of sacraments from the point of view of their effect on man, rather than as they proceeded, so to speak, from the hand of God. And so he maintained that

THE MIDDLE AGES 129

the way in which they work is to produce a certain disposition in the soul which of necessity calls forth grace direct from God. But a disposition in the soul is as much a spiritual effect as any other, and he abandoned this explanation for one more subtle but more complete.

Going back to God as the true source of all grace, he showed how God had used the suffering humanity of Christ as His direct instrument in applying His grace to human kind. The sacraments, as links with the incarnate Son of God, were secondary instruments for the conferring of this grace. An illustrative figure would be that of a man felling a tree. The man himself is the cause of the action, but his arm is a primary instrument and the axe is a secondary instrument. So God uses the human nature of Christ as an immediate instrument (conjunctum) and the sacraments as a separate instrument (disjunctum) of His action. Thus if the sacraments were to such early Fathers as Ignatius and Irenaeus extensions of the Resurrection, they are now viewed, in the well-known phrase, as extensions of the Incarnation. True, this does not really explain how material things can be the causes of spiritual, but it guards against low forms of the belief that they are, and it retains the religiously all-important view of sacraments as real causes of grace. This continued to be the generally received teaching of the Church until the Council of Trent which, in its seventh session, made it authoritative, in the full sense that sacraments contain the grace they signify, and actually confer it upon those whose disposition presents no obstacle to receiving it.

But scholastic theology was not yet satisfied. Granted that the sacraments were true causes of grace, there were yet two orders of causality, physical and moral. To which order did sacramental causality belong ? If to the former, it would imply that contact with the sacraments would infallibly confer grace upon the suitably disposed ; if to the latter, it would imply that reception of the sacraments inevitably moved God to confer grace. The latter theory was adopted by the Scotists, but it was easy to reply to them that their theory reduced the sacraments to the level of acted prayers. Yet every theologian felt the difficulty involved in making grace subject to matter. However, the Jesuit Suarez argued for physical causation on the ground that everything is capable of fulfilling the end designed for it by the Creator, and that therefore even the material elements in the sacraments may, in obedience to their determined end, infuse grace. Roman Catholic opinion is still divided upon the subject. The *Catholic Encyclopedia* adopts the view of Suarez, but a recent writer, Billot, has effected a return to the other view, and regards the devout reception of the sacraments as conferring a ' title ' to grace.[1]

It is interesting and illuminating to find a wide divergence of opinion among scholars of unimpeachable orthodoxy upon so important a matter, and it should give pause to those who think that ' Modernist '

[1] See T. A. Lacey in *E.R.E.*, art. ' Sacraments.'

difficulties must of necessity invalidate the whole theory of sacraments. Yet it may be doubted whether the difficulty will long continue to be felt by thinkers who accept a spiritual view of the universe. It is obvious that the controversy rests upon a sharp division between matter and spirit. But scholars who take account of the recent researches in bio-chemistry and psychology, and quite ordinary people who meditate upon the mystery of human birth sometimes find that hard line of demarcation softened almost to the point of disappearance. With its disappearance the difficulty about a 'quasi-physical' view of the sacraments would disappear also.

3

In its initial stages the controversy about the efficacy of the sacraments was undoubtedly complicated by the prevailing indecision as to their number, which involved a certain amount of doubt as to what precisely a sacrament meant. In this respect also the Middle Ages introduce us to a process of delimitation.

The earliest Christian Latin writers used the word 'sacrament' with great freedom. For Tertullian it can even mean the whole Christian religion. But it speedily acquired a specialized use for sacred things that have a hidden significance, as when Cyprian says that the seamless robe is a sacrament of the unity of the Church. Even Augustine still used it in a wide sense, although he had also a more specific use, as, for instance, when he contrasted the many sacraments of the Old Testament with the few of the New. This was itself a step towards confining the use of the word to certain symbolic rites of the Church.

As we have seen, the requirements of Augustine's theology led him to distinguish sharply between the sign and the thing signified. He thus passed naturally to a special distinction of certain sacraments that were the vehicles of grace. But it was long before the line was clearly drawn. Even in the twelfth century Hugh of S. Victor [1] enumerates no fewer than thirty sacraments, but he mentions seven principal ones within his larger circle. Otto of Bamberg,[2] c. 1127, seems to have been the first to give the definite number seven, but he speaks of it as already traditional. However, it was Peter Lombard in his *Sentences* who first popularized that exclusive number. His book was for many generations the received text-book of theology, and the number thus became conventional. No one could give a very satisfactory reason for it, but it received the sanction of the Orthodox Churches of the East and of S. Thomas Aquinas. The reason one would naturally allege, that seven and seven only could be justified from the New Testament, might have been accepted as final, if S. Bernard [3] had not stoutly maintained that the feet-washing was also a sacrament instituted by Christ for continuance in His Church. The number was finally fixed by the Council

---

[1] *De Sacr. Chr. Fidei.*
[2] *Sermon to Pomeranians* (*P.L.* clxxiii. 1358).
[3] *Serm. in Cena Dom.* (ed. Mabillon), p. 897.

THE MIDDLE AGES

of Trent, which condemned all who should say that there were more or less than seven. The Council's further condemnation of any who should say that not all of them were ordained by Christ Himself is an exceedingly hard saying. The only possible justification of it would be to equate all New Testament usage with the ordinance of Jesus.

If we follow the division adopted in the early chapters of this book, we shall see that all three modes of sacramentalism are represented in the seven. The Eucharist is a sacrament of object, and Penance of word. Confirmation, Orders, and Marriage are sacraments of action. Baptism and Unction properly belong also to the class of action, but in fact they have occupied an intermediary position. Originally the outward sign was recognized as the act of washing or anointing, but after the custom of hallowing the water and the oil became established, it was natural, if regrettable, that grace should be popularly and loosely held to reside within the elements so used. But, in point of fact, this kind of question was not so carefully discussed in relation to any other sacrament as to the Eucharist.

After the number of the sacraments had been fixed, many rites of the Church, which in the past had received the name of sacraments, now fell into a subordinate position. By modern theologians they are spoken of as 'sacramentals.' A well-known instance is the anointing of kings, which S. Peter Damien had included among his twelve sacraments. It is not disputed that special help may be given through such signs, but they have not the authority

SACRAMENTALISM

of the seven. If their position is somewhat ambiguous, they at least act as a useful bridge between the sacraments proper and that universal sacramentalism which would bring all outward things under bondage to Christ.

4

We return now to the greatest of the sacraments, and find the clearest process of limitation carried out during the Middle Ages not merely in the theory of 'conversion' but in the theory as to the manner of that conversion.

Medieval doctrine was developed largely as an attempt by the theologians to maintain the unique greatness of the Eucharist by explaining it from a rational point of view while avoiding the crudities of popular piety, which had early begun to interpret the conversion of the bread and wine into Flesh and Blood in the most materialistic fashion. The difficulty was to preserve at once the belief in the Real Presence and the Augustinian distinction between the sign and the thing signified. Again and again the attempt broke down, and reason proclaimed its impotence by finding resort in a miracle or in a confession of ignorance. A way out, which proved ultimately something in the nature of an 'impasse,' seemed to be offered by the development of the Realistic philosophy with its distinction between 'substance'—the inner reality—and 'accidents'—the attributes by which this reality made itself known to the senses.

THE MIDDLE AGES

In 844, Paschasius Radbert, a monk of Corbie, published his book *On the Body and Blood of the Lord*, in which he explained that the change of the bread and wine into the flesh and blood of Christ is an inward one, not apparent to sight or touch. This is possible only by a fresh miraculous creation. Nevertheless, the Eucharistic body is truly identical with the historical body of Christ, and the non-apparent character of the change is meant to call forth our faith and to prevent us from regarding the gift as other than spiritual. A fellow-monk of Corbie, Ratramn, called upon by King Charles to offer his comments upon this, denied a change of substance; in actual substance the elements remain the same, but they acquire the spiritual power and effect of the body and blood of Christ. So far from being identical with the historical body of Christ they are but the pledge and image of it.

Authority, however, favoured Paschasius, and popular thought continued on its materialistic way, going so far as to claim that the consecrated species was incorruptible, thus proving itself the actual material flesh of Christ. If the bread became the material flesh of Christ it was natural to hold that His very flesh was pressed by the teeth of the wicked as well as the good. Such superstitions brought forth the rebuke of Berengar of Tours, who in his book on the *Holy Supper* (1073) brought his trained dialectical skill to bear on the question, and contended that 'accidents' cannot exist without a subject. The elements of bread and wine, therefore, do not cease to exist—consecration does not destroy but enhances that which is consecrated—yet every sacrament implies a 'thing signified,' and it is this inner reality that is received. What, therefore, the faithful receive is not a particle of flesh but the whole Christ, and Him they do not receive with their mouth but with their heart, and consequently the wicked do not receive Him at all. Berengar was forced to retract, but some parts of his teaching remained the possession of the later Schoolmen, and in spite of the opposition of our own Lanfranc discussion was henceforth conducted on a more spiritual level. It is usually held that a permanent witness to the defeat of Berengarius is to be found in the elevation of the Host immediately after the words, 'This is My Body.'

The effort to retain the real but spiritual values of the Mass was continued by Peter Lombard, who, while clinging to the view of conversion, is clear that the accidents remain, and that there is no fraction of the Lord's body. He argues that the change of substance takes place not by special creation, not by annihilation, nor by addition, but by 'transition.' Thus the whole Christ is received, but He is received by faith, so that, although the wicked may receive sacramentally, they do not receive spiritually. Yet it is said that this same Lombard, when asked what happened if a beast ate this sacrament with its one divine substance, could only answer, 'God knows.'

The language of transubstantiation was first used authoritatively by the Fourth Council of the Lateran in 1215, which stated that 'His body and blood are really contained in the Sacrament of the Altar under the species of bread and wine, the bread being transubstantiated into the Body, and the wine into the Blood, by the power of God.' This has ever since been the official teaching of the Roman Church, being repeated still more definitely by the Council of Trent. It was also accepted in effect by the Greek Church at the Council of Lyons in 1274. Some further examination of it was made by Thomas Aquinas, who came to the conclusion that the *whole* Christ was present in *each* species by ' concomitance ' and in every fragment of each species ; that the Body remains until the species becomes corrupt ; and that the presence of Christ in the sacrament is not a local presence in the sense that Christ Himself is moved as the sacrament is moved. He is present as in a sign, not as in a vessel. These are conclusions of the greatest importance for a spiritual view. But S. Thomas feels acutely the difficulty of the accidents. How could they function without a subject ? No answer seems possible, and under the fierce questioning of such skilled debaters as Occam and Wycliffe the philosophical theory upon which medieval sacramental doctrine was built up began to show signs of breaking in pieces. It was left for faith to accept what reason had in the last resort been unable to prove.

.   .   .   .

It is hoped that this rapid sketch of medieval sacramental theology will have sufficed to show the steps by which the issues were made clear, and the question how sacraments work could be squarely faced. Once the sacraments were definitely limited

SACRAMENTALISM

in number it became easy to apply the Augustinian distinction between the sign and the thing signified. After this the difficulties would not have been great if it could have been maintained that the Eucharist was a sacrament similar in kind to all the rest. Sacraments of action and of word did not bring into too close a relationship the spiritual and the physical. But it was just because the Eucharist was regarded as a sacrament of object that the difficulty of the association between material and spiritual was seen to be acute, and henceforth attention was concentrated upon this point. The one thing definitely inherited from earlier ages was the complete assurance that here, through and by means of the material elements, man had access to something more than a power of God, and that here, as in the Incarnation itself:

> A higher gift than grace
> Could flesh and blood refine,
> God's presence, and His very self
> And essence all divine.

But how could this stupendous thing come to pass through such beggarly means ? Two views emerged. Both agreed that the consecrated Sacrament is the body and blood of Christ ; they differed in their explanation. ' The one group maintains that the Eucharist is like the Incarnation, and the consecrated Sacrament like the incarnate life of the Lord, so that, as in the incarnate life, the Godhead and the manhood are both there and both unchanged; similarly in the consecrated Sacrament the bread and wine continue to exist in all their reality, while

THE MIDDLE AGES

there is also the body and blood of the Lord.[1] The other group minimizes the continuance of the bread and wine, and lays stress on the change by which the elements are re-ordered or transferred or transformed or transmade into the body and blood.'[2] The theory ultimately accepted was that of Transubstantiation, the replacing of the essence of the material bread and wine by the essential being of the Incarnate. Under the terms of the received philosophy of the day it was perhaps the best theory that could be framed. But the average mind was never able to grasp it. For the many it merely meant an assurance that what they took into their mouths was the material flesh of the Saviour which had suffered upon the Cross. To what extravagance this led must be realized by every one who reads Mr. Coulton's *Five Centuries of Religion*, extravagance so great as to make possible the hope expressed in Browning's fearful line, ' To see God made and eaten all day long.'

But it was precisely this materialism that the theory was framed to make impossible. For the philosopher it was as purely spiritual a conception as could be formed. Yet even for him it proved no haven of refuge. This is shown quite clearly by the controversy about causality—a controversy far more important for modern minds than the dogma of Transubstantiation itself. Does physical contact with the outward sign convey to us the inestimable gift, or does it merely constitute a moral claim upon

[1] See this worked out in interesting article by Relton, *C.Q.R.* (April 1928).
[2] Stone, *Anglo-Catholic Report*, p. 103.

SACRAMENTALISM

God, whereby He must, in obedience to His own pledge, bestow the gift upon our souls ? That is a question that still remains unanswered, and it goes deeper into the roots of things than anything settled at the Council of Trent.

Even so there was still another difficulty for the Transubstantiation theory, caused by the characteristic thought-forms of the day. When people naturally thought of heaven as being primarily a place, and of risen bodies as being subject to the same spatial and temporal limitations as beset the body before death, what was to be said of the body of Christ ? If it is seated at the right hand of God, how can it be at the same time upon the altar or upon many altars ? That is a question that became important during the Reformation, and perhaps of all the questions then raised it is the one that will make us feel that even in the midst of that great upheaval we have not passed altogether out of the medieval atmosphere.

But in general we may say that at the opening of the sixteenth century the philosophic difficulties were thrown into the shade by the confirmed and unanimous materialism of popular views. It was against this that the Reformation provided a violent reaction. Study of the New Testament and the Greek Fathers, as well as the somewhat sceptical attitude induced by the Renaissance, made impossible for thinking people the easy certainty of the ' Age of Faith.' The bond of the old authority once cast aside, the way was open for a fresh consideration of the whole subject of sacraments.

CHAPTER XI

THE REFORMATION AND AFTER

THE medieval presentation of Christianity has been accused of being a system that sought ' salvation by means of sacraments.' The effect of the Reformation, at least on the Continent, was to produce an essentially non-sacramental religion, a system in which the sacraments were merely ' optional appendages ' to religion. The most obvious and immediate change was the reduction of the number of the sacraments from seven to two. Upon this reduction there was a fairly general agreement, although Penance was some time in being dropped. But there the agreement ended. In the discussion of sacramental method bitter controversy arose, and a kind of Hegelian thesis, antithesis, and synthesis was formed by the teaching of Luther, Zwingli, and Calvin.

I

As a religious leader Luther is one of the greatest figures in Christian history : as a theologian he is variable, ambiguous, and confused. In 1520 he held to three sacraments—Baptism, Penance, and Bread—but later he supported only Baptism and Bread, giving as the reason that in these two alone

142 SACRAMENTALISM

do we find the divinely instituted sign and the promise of forgiveness. For his rationale of the sacraments he went back beyond scholastic teaching to Augustine, finding his most fruitful suggestion in the latter's description of the sacraments as ' visible words.' As such they ' individualize' the promise made generally in God's Word. Here, then, begins that emphasis upon words which in the Protestant system replaces the Catholic emphasis on sacraments. To the Reformers words were all-important, whether in the Bible or in the pulpit or in the liturgy. The grace received in the sacrament is the same as that received in the hearing of the word, but ' a man can have and use the word or testament without the sign or sacrament.' Luther draws a valuable distinction between sacrament and sacrifice. In sacrifice man offers something to God ; in a sacrament God does all. Even faith contributes nothing to the efficacy of a sacrament, although it is necessary for the appropriation of the gift.[1]

These principles seem to work radically. Thus in Baptism it is not the water that produces a spiritual effect, but the word of God, which accompanies and is connected with the water, and our faith, which relies on the word of God connected with the water. Similarly in the Mass it is not the eating and drinking but ' the words which stand here : " given and shed for you for the remission of sins." [2] . . . He who believes these words has what they set forth, namely, the remission of sins.' Thus the conception of sacramental grace as that which brings us into vital

---
[1] Cf. Jacobs, *E.R.E.* x. 909.　　[2] Short catechism.

relation with the whole personality of the living Christ—the conception which lay behind the thinking of the Greek Fathers and of the best of the Schoolmen—is here replaced by the one gift of the forgiveness of sins. Yet so strong were the associations of Luther's early life that by a curious inconsistency he clings whole-heartedly to a belief in the Real Presence, rejecting indeed the Transubstantiation theory but replacing it by a theory of Consubstantiation not unlike that of Berengarius, namely, that after the consecration there are two substances within the elements, that of bread and wine and that of the body and blood of the Lord. This came about because he would not explain away the words of institution. It is well known how at the Marburg Conference of 1529, when the Lord's Supper was under discussion by the rival schools of reformers, he chalked on the table before him the words 'This is My Body' and rigidly refused to retreat from that simple statement.

2

A very different type of thinker was Zwingli, pushing principles to their logical conclusion, and having at least the merit of striving to consider scriptural passages in their historical setting. Unfortunately he had no adequate resources for conjuring up the historical setting of the Last Supper. Consequently he rejected the literal interpretation of the words of institution, and said that the word 'is' meant no more than 'signifies,' adducing the unfortunate parallel of a woman who should point to her wedding-ring and say, ' This is my husband.'[1] There is thus no need to think of eating even a ' spiritual ' body ; all a sacrament does is to bear public witness to the fact that grace has already been given. ' All sacraments are so far from conferring grace that they do not even bring or dispense it.'[2] The Lord's Supper is ' nothing else than a commemoration.'

3

Between these warring opinions, Calvin, the great systematic theologian, tried to effect some kind of reconciliation. He accepted the Lutheran connexion between words and sacraments, and explained the latter as visible tokens or pledges of God's promises, like the seal appended to a student's diploma.[3] With Zwingli he objects to the theory of a ' secret efficacy perpetually inherent in the sacraments,' and states that they do not of themselves bestow any grace, but they ' announce and manifest it.' The teaching that ' the sacraments of the New Law justify and confer grace, provided only that we do not interpose the obstacle of mortal sin,' he regards as being ' plainly of the devil.'

Yet he will not go all the way with Zwingli in saying that the only effect of sacraments is to bear public witness to our confession, but holds that the more important effect is actually to contribute to our faith. On the other hand, he uncompromisingly

[1] *Opera* (ed. 1581), ii. 293 ; cf. 209.
[2] *Ibid.* 541.   [3] *Institutes*, iv. ch. xiv. sec. 5.

rejects Luther's consubstantiation theory. Luther had been able to defend his view on the ground of his belief that the ubiquity of Christ's divinity had been communicated to His humanity, so that His body could be in many places at once. Calvin regards Christ's body as being in Heaven : it cannot therefore be on any altar, but it can be and is received by the faithful communicant. How this can be he does not know. 'I shall not be ashamed to confess that it is a mystery too sublime for me. . . . I rather experience than understand it.'[1] This is the doctrine generally known as Receptionism, its watchword has in modern times become 'Christ not on the altar or in the hand, but in the heart.'

4

The position of the Church of England in these matters was not, as is sometimes said, a *via media*, but an effort at comprehension. After hesitating between various ways of presenting sacramental doctrine, it made a determined effort to provide a home for all who were not bound to Zwingli's commemoration theory on the one hand, or to a materialistic view of transubstantiation on the other. It abandoned all strictness of philosophic interpretation and returned to the freedom of the primitive church. 'What shocks us about the Church of England,' a recent French writer has said, 'is that it embraces such wide divergences of doctrine.' But it is questionable whether some measure of diversity is not

[1] Cf. xvii. 31, 32.

146   SACRAMENTALISM

nearer to the spirit of the New Testament than the subtlety of definition actually enforced in some other parts of Christendom.

In addition to adopting this wide view of sacramental theory the Church of England endeavoured also to preserve a just balance between the sacraments and the emotional and moral aspects of religion. That it was sorely tempted to let the sacraments fall into the non-essential class of religious observance is a matter of common knowledge, but not many perhaps remember Donne's magnificent reply to the whole Puritan attack upon outward rites : ' Beloved, outward things apparel God, and since God was content to take a body, let us not leave Him naked and ragged.' Few who have used the Prayer Book as a whole could accuse it of representing a non-sacramental religion, while the Articles, with all their faults, at least prevent any over-stressing of the institutional side of Christianity. That our formularies do not show precisely the same emphasis in every part can easily be proved, but to point out the same phenomenon in the official forms and pronouncements of all other churches provides the entertainment of most modern historical theologians.

In estimating the number of the sacraments the English Church gave a needed distinction to the two ordained by Christ Himself. But the five others, commonly (though not unjustifiably) called sacraments, were all given a place in the First Prayer Book, and only Unction was afterwards omitted, probably because the common way of celebrating it had departed from apostolic example and made the last

THE REFORMATION AND AFTER 147

of the anointings into ' Extreme Unction.' In spite of Puritan efforts the others were retained, and it was replied to all attacks at the Savoy Conference that, ' our Church doth everywhere conform to the Catholic usages of the primitive times, from which causelessly to depart argues rather love of contention than of peace.' Thus the standard showed no wide divergence from that of the best Roman tradition. The greater prominence given to the two Gospel sacraments might easily have been defended by the Council of Trent, which expressly condemned the teaching that all sacraments were of the same value.

In its explanation of the way in which sacraments work, the English Church followed S. Augustine, and indeed its theology represents a return to S. Augustine on both sides of his teaching. Thus Article XXV asserts that ' sacraments ordained of Christ be not only badges or tokens . . . but rather . . . effectual signs of grace,' that is to say, they actually bring the grace they signify. Similarly the Catechism distinguishes in Augustinian fashion between the outward, visible sign and the inward, spiritual grace. And Hooker uses the relation between soul and body in man as a parallel to the relation between the unseen and the seen in the Sacrament.

How far did this involve a belief in the Real Presence in the Eucharist ? There was a bad moment in 1552 when the Council of Edward VI held up the publication of the Second Prayer Book in order to insert in it, against Cranmer's will and without ecclesiastical sanction, the 'Black Rubric,' which explained the practice of kneeling at communion as not meaning that 'any adoration is done, or ought to be done, either unto the sacramental bread or wine there bodily received, or to any real and essential presence there being of Christ's natural flesh and blood.' So hastily was the thing done that some copies of the book got out without it, and in others it was only pasted in on a fly-sheet. And, in any case, it did not last, for at the next revision it was omitted altogether, and when it was reintroduced in 1662 the words 'real and essential' had been replaced by 'corporal.' Thus what was denied was a material presence, and a real but spiritual presence was by implication allowed.

The mode of that Presence was happily left undefined. There is, in Article XXVIII, a definite repudiation of the Transubstantiation theory. But as we have already seen, that theory is itself capable of different interpretations. The greater schoolmen used it to oppose materialistic conceptions. If 'substance' can only be grasped by the mind, then all that is material in the bread and wine remain after consecration as before. But this was too refined for the majority, and for them the 'conversion' theory still implied that the bread became the body of Christ in such a sense that, for instance, the Host, when broken, might bleed. It is doubtless in this sense that the doctrine was rejected. As thus interpreted it would indeed overthrow the nature of a sacrament, because it would leave after consecration not two things, an outward and an inward, but one, and it would be repugnant to the plain words of Scripture, which still call that which is eaten by the communicant 'bread.'[1] But it must be admitted that the doctrine was reasserted in uncompromising terms at the thirteenth session of the Council of Trent in October 1551. This was more than a year before the publication of the English articles in 1553, and it is consequently disputed whether the English article has the Tridentine definition in view or not.

In any case we may take it that what is condemned by the Article is a particular interpretation of a particular theory. In a country where the word 'substance' has acquired, in everyday use, the sense of matter, that condemnation has certainly been valuable in guarding against superstition. Yet when the word is used in its philosophical sense as employed by the schoolmen to denote 'the impalpable universal which was held to inhere in every particular included under it,' it actually destroys that very materialism which its popular use would seem to set up. Even so the English Church has done wisely in not confining herself to that or any other definition that depends upon a precise philosophic theory. Systems of philosophy, like other systems, have their day and cease to be. They are useful as the handmaids of theology, but theology stultifies herself if she becomes the slave of any. They help her to state her revealed truth in the terms of the knowledge of the day, but her truth remains long after their usefulness has ceased. The shifts

[1] I Cor. xi. 26, 28.

SACRAMENTALISM

to which a thinker may be put when he has to accept a truth of religion stated in the terms of an outworn philosophy may be illustrated from the attitude of Newman to this very question of transubstantiation : ' Why should it not be ? What's to hinder it ? . . . It deals with what no one on earth knows anything about, the material substances themselves.'[1]

We may sum up the results of the Reformation controversies by saying that out of the welter of opinions five principal views emerged. ' Transubstantiation was one of them. Belief in the presence of our Lord's body and blood in the consecrated sacrament, together with the continued existence of the whole substance of bread and wine, was another. The opinion that the consecrated Sacrament itself is no more than bread and wine, but that the faithful communicant at the moment of reception inwardly receives the body and blood of Christ, was a third. A fourth was that the faithful communicant receives, not the body and blood of Christ themselves, but their virtue and power. According to a fifth, the Eucharist is a merely symbolical rite, a remembrance of the past.'[2]

Of these the English Church condemns the last and at least a crude interpretation of the first. In the Roman Church, on the other hand, there have been two different reactions to the doctrine of Transubstantiation. While many writers have sought to make the dogma more acceptable by insisting upon the abiding reality of the accidents

---
[1] *Apologia* (1864), pp. 374–5.
[2] Stone, *Anglo-Catholic Report*, 105.

of the bread and wine, the Sacred Congregation in 1875 actually sharpened the traditional view by condemning certain teaching that seemed to tone down the conversion of the whole substance of the elements.[1] The Eastern Church to-day would probably find it difficult to accept this sharpened definition of Transubstantiation. Dr. Pullan[2] sums up the present attitude of the Orthodox as follows : 'The whole Eastern Church has adopted words equivalent to transubstantiation, while not investing them with the highest authority and while repudiating a material or, as the Greeks say, ' physicochemical' sense of the word. And the Slavs, not the Greeks, decline to employ the word ' accidents ' in connexion with their doctrine of transubstantiation. All the Eastern Orthodox declare that the mystery passes human understanding, and that to explain perfectly the manner of the change is impossible.'

It will be seen, then, that neither the Reformation nor the subsequent period produced any satisfactory explanation of this great mystery. From the point of view of the philosophy in which it was framed, consubstantiation seemed frankly impossible : it was more difficult to think of two different substances inhering at the same time within one set of accidents than to think of the substance being changed while the accidents remained the same. Zwinglianism, receptionism, virtualism suffered from the graver disadvantage that they ignored the distinctive character of the Eucharist as an object

[1] Stone, *Doctrine of Holy Eucharist*, ii. 415–6.
[2] *Religion since the Reformation*, p. 206.

SACRAMENTALISM

sacrament. To refuse to recognize in it this character was to reject the lesson of history, but in days when the faculty of criticism was only struggling to the birth, judgments were perforce more subjective than historical, and in face of the great abuses in which a whole-hearted recognition of the 'object' character of the Eucharistic sacrament had been involved, it was natural that there should be a reaction in favour of what seemed less materialistic views. However, on the interpretation of the history adopted in this book, the greater measure of truth lay with the other side. In the sacraments, as in other respects, the new dispensation was the heir of the old. Jesus accepted the object mode of sacramentalism, as He did the others, giving to it also a new meaning and a richness of content derived from the uniqueness of His own personality. This view involves the belief that the presence of the Lord is directly associated with the bread and wine. They who hold it are divided into two groups, as they believe that the substance of the bread and wine does or does not remain after the consecration. Whether the difference between them is as great or as important as is sometimes supposed, may be doubted. ' For my part,' says Dr. Stone, ' I do not think the difference between the two devotionally or spiritually important. . . . What in my judgment is important for the Christian soul is not whether the substance of bread and wine is absent, but whether the Lord is present.' [1] With that judgment we cordially agree.

[1] *Anglo-Catholic Congress Report*, p. 106.

CHAPTER XII

MODERN VIEWS AND DIFFICULTIES

WE have now traced the course of sacramentalism from its beginning in primitive religion through the history of the Jewish and Christian Churches down to modern times. Our effort has been to show the continuity of this belief, and in order to do this it has been necessary to describe the many ways in which men have conceived that material things may be the means of communicating spiritual gifts. We saw that there can be distinguished three main modes of sacramentalism in which spirit uses respectively object, action, and word. But over and above these three modes there are the many efforts that have been made to give a reasonable explanation of the way in which material substance itself may convey spiritual gifts. This has been the more debated inasmuch as many who find no difficulty in the thought of God making direct use of human actions or words find it quite incredible that He should associate Himself with any material object.

Yet, as we have seen, belief in such an association is common to all the ages. Indeed, it is interesting to observe how the same cycle of ideas that can be found in early religious history is repeated, though, of course, with greater refinement, in the history of Christianity. The progress of sacramentalism might be represented as a spiral. We begin with the practical identification of spirit with matter in the primitive ' eating of the god,' and work up through the association of the life with the blood to the notion of a spiritual efficacy that hovered more and more faintly about certain sacred rites in the late pre-Christian period. This was reinforced by influences that may have been ultimately derived from the atmosphere surrounding the mystery cults. The widely diffused sacramental view was accepted by Jesus, and its force was directed under His inspiration into certain definite channels. Starting from Him, the curve of Christian sacramentalism describes much the same contour as, but on a higher level than, the pre-Christian, the chief points in the progress being the mystical and incarnational interpretation of the Greek Fathers, and the theories of consubstantiation and transubstantiation. When we come to the materialistic view of the last-named doctrine, we find ourselves parallel to the point at which we started.

But however it worked, that matter was a possible vehicle of spirit no one in antiquity, not even the Hebrew prophets, seems to have doubted. Jesus, as we have seen, used it and allowed its use for His purpose. It might conceivably be questioned whether in this He was simply making a concession to popular ideas or was lending His authority to an age-long method, were it not that the solemnity attending the Last Supper and the witness of the early Church, as evidenced by the New Testament writers, forbid the former conclusion and make inevitable the latter. Nevertheless there are certain presuppositions that are strong enough in the minds of many to overcome even this great authority and to make impossible a belief in sacramental grace. With those presuppositions we propose to deal before the close. But in the meantime we may round off our consideration of sacramental method by asking whether any of the theories hitherto expounded is completely satisfactory. The fact is that sooner or later they all come to a point where a direct act of God must be called in to fill the gap left by human knowledge. The various speculations along Aristotelian lines have indeed been of inestimable service in making clear the issues and pointing out the dangers on either side. But it is questionable whether at the moment any further advance can be made by travelling in the old ways.

I

This does not point to a failure in theology but in philosophy. It may be doubted whether the weapons in the philosopher's armoury are any longer effective. At present there is a good deal of dissatisfaction in more than one sphere of thought with the category of substance. Some theologians allege, for instance, that it has led to an impasse in the field of christology. If they begin with two distinct substances, one of divinity and the other of humanity, they find it impossible to demonstrate logically how both can be united in the one Person of Christ. This has induced them to try another road along the line of ' value ' judgments, showing that the one Christ has the values both of God and man. This is parallel with an attempt to appreciate the sacraments in accordance with their psychological values.

Three interesting attempts have recently been made by English writers of repute to interpret the Eucharist on these lines. The first is by the Bishop of Manchester,[1] who suggests the term ' convaluation ' to explain the fact of the Real Presence. ' That,' he says, ' is " present " which is apprehensible. The Eucharistic Bread has the double value of enabling us to apprehend both the bread which nourishes the body and the Christ who is the food of the soul. Hence the two values, material and spiritual, are present together in the sacrament, and justify the use of the term convaluation.' This explanation is coupled with a difficult stressing of the Pauline phrase ' Body of Christ,' as applied to the Church in much the same sense as to the sacrament,[2] and there is added an unfortunate denial that the Eucharistic Body is identical with the Body of flesh and blood risen, ascended, and glorified.[3] ' Our contention is that when S. Paul called the Church the Body of Christ he used the words in just the same sense as when he called the Eucharistic Bread the Body of Christ.' Yet Dr. Temple's devotional language is unexceptionable : ' When in faith you receive the Bread and the Wine you receive the

---

[1] Temple, *Christus Veritas*, 15, 239-52.
[2] Op. cit. 250, 251.   [3] Op. cit. 246.

MODERN VIEWS AND DIFFICULTIES 157

Lord Jesus Christ into your soul as truly as those who opened their doors to Him in Palestine received Him into their homes.'[1]

Another attempt is that made by Mr. Will Spens in *Essays Catholic and Critical*.[2] He accepts the term 'convaluation,' but prefers 'transvaluation.' He defines an object as 'a complex of persisting opportunities of experience.' The Eucharistic Bread offers a double set of such opportunities : we experience contact with bread and also with the Incarnate Son of God. But as in handling a florin we think not of the natural properties of the silver but of the purchasing value of the coin, so in the Eucharist the conception of the Body supersedes that of the bread. This change in experience is so fundamental that it justifies us in calling the Bread quite simply the Body of Christ. We ought not to speak even of a 'sacramental Body' lest we seem to teach a 'multi-corporal' Christ. 'In the only sense in which we can still think of our Lord's glorified body as identical with His natural body, we must think of His sacramental body as identical with that body.' Thus the bread and the wine are given, by Christ's ordinance, new properties, which, while they do not annihilate the natural properties of giving sustenance and refreshment, yet so supersede them that we can rightly speak of the elements as wholly changed and transfigured. This is an extremely interesting and illuminating theory. Yet in the last resort it depends on the psychological 'opportunity of experience,' and does not probe to the very nature of the real

[1] Op. cit. 252 n. [2] Pp. 439–45.

158 SACRAMENTALISM

thing, and it may be doubted whether its scholastic equivalent is as necessarily transubstantiation as its author supposes.

A third view has recently been put forward which shows much sympathy with those who think in terms of value judgments, while revealing marked divergences from the two views already considered. This is to be found in the elaborate discussion by Canon Quick in his book *The Christian Sacraments*. Starting from a definition of sacrament as being not only an effective symbol but also an instrument of the divine working, he proceeds to show how the perfect example of both aspects is to be found in the life of Christ. The Christian rites commonly called sacraments are extensions both of the Incarnation and of the Atonement, for whereas divine self-expression is summed up in the Incarnation, divine operation is summed up in the Atonement. Thus when he comes to the Eucharist the writer considers that the consecrated elements may as rightly be called ' significant instruments ' as ' effectual signs.' This leads him to emphasize the use of the sacrament at the expense of the sacrament itself. ' The presence is to be sought in the elements not as physical objects, but as they are within the process of a certain action which takes them up into itself, uses them as its instruments, and expresses itself in them.' Again, ' As regards the effect of consecration, there seems to be no reason why we should not willingly accept the statement that the bread and wine are changed so as to become the Body and Blood of Christ, if it be understood that the terms body and blood denote, not

MODERN VIEWS AND DIFFICULTIES 159

material things as such, but outward things as they are in relation to a spiritual activity which operates and expresses itself through them.' One is in doubt here in what sense the writer is using the word 'activity.' Body and blood are surely the means of expression used by a person and not merely by an 'activity,' but one suspects that the word is here used almost as the equivalent of 'action.' The suspicion is deepened even by so carefully guarded a statement as the following, ' It may be true to say that the presence resides in what is done with the elements rather than in the elements themselves, if it be remembered that in the process of that action the elements are more than merely the instruments of a living spirit beyond them, and become actually the expression of the life of that spirit itself.' Naturally after this Canon Quick is constrained to say, ' We here definitely part company with S. Thomas when he differentiates between the Eucharist and other sacraments by saying that " this sacrament is accomplished in the consecration of the matter, whereas other sacraments are accomplished in the use of the consecrated matter." '[1] This shows quite clearly the true character of the explanation. It is an attempt to mediate between the 'object' and 'action' theories of the mode of this sacrament, but in the end it can only find peace by abandoning the former. It is really impossible to combine object with action in the case of the Eucharist, unless we recognize that it must first become the Body of the Divine Person before it can be His instrument. In

[1] Pp. 225-6.

the Eucharist there are quite distinct and separate moments, and one is compelled to ask, What on this theory is the condition of the consecrated elements between the consecration and the communion? To believe that the Presence is somehow incomplete until the moment of reception is to fall back into Calvinism, however strong is the affirmation of the Real Presence. Nevertheless, by his very valuable insistence upon the sacraments as instruments of the divine working, Canon Quick has done much to restore to the Eucharist its dynamic character, and to remove the reproach of materialism which is apt to settle upon it when it is viewed too statically as merely a shrine of the sacramental presence.

2

What is needed by the ordinary person is some explanation that will be reasonable and preserve the religious values while not trespassing too much upon the ground of philosophy. He will find means ready to his hand in the doctrine of grace. Rightly interpreted this will keep him in touch with that more strictly personal mode of expression which is proper to the sphere of religion. It will help him to realize that for him the important thing is not so much the distinction between the sign and the thing signified (upon which our own catechism has laid so great a stress), but the wide difference between the sacrament and the virtue of the sacrament.

Grace, then, is the free and undeserved help of God. It is not really some quasi-fluid substance that can

MODERN VIEWS AND DIFFICULTIES 161

flow through a channel, nor a power like that of electricity that can pass along a wire, although such metaphors seem to be indispensable in our descriptions of its working. It is God acting in His bountiful loving-kindness towards the sons of men : God's personal benevolence acting upon the individual. This the Father showed uniquely in the Incarnation of His eternal Son. Grace came by Jesus Christ : in Him the kindness and love of God appeared. This was the supreme Sacrament, for in it the Creator took part of His universe, the human flesh and blood derived from Mary, to convey His gifts to men. Looking upon the universe as it is revealed in this example, we are able to perceive in it as a whole a vast sacrament of God's love. His mercy is over all His works, and the natural world is a garment that reveals even while it conceals the form of its Creator.

Obviously there are some parts and elements of this universe that are more fitted to reveal Him than others. Of these our Saviour used the most easily adaptable to continue the method of the Incarnation after His own visible presence was withdrawn from the earth. To explain His relation to the Bread and Wine we need to remember that He called them His Body and Blood, and that we ourselves are quite familiar with the relation between invisible personalities and the outward bodies that give them the opportunity of self-expression and of communication with others. It is true that the Bread is inanimate while our bodies are animate. But we may reasonably take the Lord's relation to the sacramental Bread as equivalent to that between soul and body.

And we shall be saved from all spatial crudities and helped to remember that the Presence is there as ' in a sign rather than as in a vessel ' if we remember that we really do not know with regard even to ourselves whether our souls are in our bodies or our bodies in our souls. Such a view will also preserve our sense of proportion in all discussions about what is ' real ' in the Eucharist. For our bodies have a merely contingent reality as compared with the soul or spirit that expresses itself through them. So although the sacramental veils of bread and wine are as real as the material bodies that receive them, this is but a temporary and shadowy reality as compared with that of the Body and Blood of Christ given by means of them.

Further, as a person not only *is*, but also speaks and acts, so there will naturally be sacramental means by which the divine-human Person of the Christ can outwardly speak and act for the comprehension of His people. The limitation of these to seven as specially ordained appears completely justified by New Testament usage. But it does not exclude the possibility of the use for a similar purpose of many other outward signs. Indeed, we may say that the supreme value of the sacramental system thus divinely ordained is that it peoples the whole material universe with the presence of God. Without the sacraments we might deride the feeling of such a pervading Presence as mere poetic fancy, and feel ourselves compelled by the logic of facts to suppose a complete separation between matter and spirit, and to think of God as a kind of absentee landlord parted by an impassable gulf from the world which He once built and still owns. But with the sacraments we have a guarantee of His abiding presence.

This, then, is the answer to those who object to sacraments on the ground that to associate God with material elements is to offer an affront to the Divine Majesty. There is, in fact, no insult here. To regard God as pure spirit incapable of contact with matter is to place Him in an empyrean in which the whole history of revelation teaches us that He does not wish to dwell. Such a view is bound to land us ultimately in a philosophic Dualism or a practical Manichæism. God is not majesty only: He is primarily love, and love must mingle freely with the creatures it has made.

But what of the objection that the teaching of sacraments is contrary to morality? If we teach 'salvation by sacraments,' is that not to dispense people from the obligation of trying to do good? Yes, if it is badly taught, but we must remember that such has never been the teaching of the Church. We recall at once Augustine's argument about efficacy: 'they cannot have the grace of God who do not love the unity of God.' And the great theologians of the Middle Ages always taught that mortal sin offers an effectual bar to the working of sacramental grace. The *ex opere operato* doctrine of the sacraments does not mean that they mechanically confer upon the recipient a title to salvation; it simply means, and always has meant, that the value of the sacraments does not depend upon the goodness of the person who ministers them—a most wholesome and necessary doctrine. The truth is that sacraments of themselves do not make any one morally better. What they do is to place in our grasp a power of God which we must use. Perhaps there would have been less misunderstanding on this head if the teaching of the Middle Ages had been put positively instead of negatively. It is not enough to say that there must be no bar to the working of grace, we must have the definite intention of putting it to the proof in the trials of daily life.[1] It is the cheque, drawn by God Himself, representing only potential wealth until we cash it and use it.

Finally there is the objection that the teaching of sacraments is in opposition to that of faith as the mainspring of the Christian life. But is that really so ? S. Paul was the great protagonist in the struggle between faith and works. Yet to him Baptism was the necessary and inevitable consequence of Christian faith. To ask which was the immediate cause of entry upon the ' state of salvation,' the faith or the baptism, is to divorce two things which S. Paul and the Early Church kept together. People who never doubted that the Lord had ordained the sacraments were not likely to contemplate the possibility of dispensing with them. But even if we limit faith to that type of Christianity which finds its readiest access to God in prayer and Bible reading, is there still any necessary opposition between this and the sacraments ? Is it not better, and more in accordance with Christian institutions, to regard both as comple-

[1] In the case of Infant Baptism this must be the intention of the godparents.

mentary in a complete Christian life ? An analogy from nature is provided by the plant which needs both a right atmosphere and a sufficient quantity of water for perfect development. In our prayers and meditations God is about us as an atmosphere : in the sacraments He enters most intimately into our personal life. The mystics have taught us to regard our personalities as no impenetrable substances, but as accessible to invasion by the Divine Spirit. The sponge in the sea and the iron in the fire are their analogies for those who, while retaining their own individuality, are yet permeated through and through by Him in whom they consciously live. It would be the crowning glory of the history of sacramentalism if it offered some explanation of the way in which we could thus fulfil the end of our being and become one with God.

SELECTED BOOK LIST

(Only works available in English are mentioned)

General—
    HASTINGS, J., Encyclopaedia of Religion and Ethics, 1907–21 (*E.R.E.*); Dictionary of the Bible, 1898–1904 (*H.D.B.*)
    HERBERMANN, etc., Catholic Encyclopaedia, 1907–22
    Modern Churchman, October 1926
    Report of Anglo-Catholic Congress, 1927
    GARDNER, A., History of Sacrament, 1921

Pre-Christian Period—
    FRAZER, J., Folk-Law in the Old Testament, 1919
    JEVONS, F. B., Introduction to History of Religion, 1896
    LOWIE, R. H., Primitive Religion, 1925
    OTTO, R., Idea of the Holy, 1923
    ROBERTSON SMITH, Religion of the Semites (New edition by S. A. COOK, 1928)

    BARTHOLET, A., History of Hebrew Civilization, 1926
    BUDDE, K., Religion of Israel to the Exile, 1899
    BURNEY, C. F., Old Testament Theology, 1903
    LOISY, A., Religion of Israel, 1910
    SANDAY, W., Priesthood and Sacrifice, 1899
    SMITH, H. P., Religion of Israel, 1914

    BUCHANAN GRAY, Sacrifice in the Old Testament, 1925
    GAYFORD, S. C., Sacrifice and Priesthood, 1924
    JAMES, E. O., Sacrifice and Sacrament, 1927

    KENNETT, R. H., Sacrifice (pamphlet), 1925
    LEGACY OF ISRAEL (ed. BEVAN and SINGER), 1927
    Old Testament Essays (papers read before the Society for Old Testament Study), 1927
    SKINNER, J., Prophecy and Religion, 1926

SACRAMENTALISM

New Testament Period—
ANGUS, S., Mystery Religions and Christianity, 1925
HALLIDAY, W. R., Pagan Background of Early Christianity, 1925
KENNEDY, H. A. A., S. Paul and the Mystery Religions, 1913
NOCK, A. D. (important article in Essays on the Trinity and the Incarnation ; ed. A. E. J. RAWLINSON, 1928)

FAIRWEATHER, W., Background of the Gospels, 1920 ; Jesus and the Greeks, 1924
GAVIN F., Jewish Antecedents of the Christian Sacraments, 1928
GLOVER, T. R., Conflict of Religions in the Early Roman Empire, 1909
MOORE, G. F., Judaism, 1927
OESTERLEY, W. O. E., Books of the Apocrypha, 1914
OESTERLEY AND BOX, Religion and Worship of the Synagogue, 1911 ; Rabbinical and Mediaeval Judaism, 1920

ABRAHAMS, I., Studies in Pharisaism and the Gospels, 1917
BARNES, W. E., Last Supper and Lord's Supper, 1927
EDERSHEIM, A., Life and Times of Jesus the Messiah, 1883
Essays Catholic and Critical (ed. E. G. SELWYN), 1926
HEADLAM, A. C., Life and Teaching of Jesus Christ, 1923
KENNETT, R. H., The Last Supper : Its Significance in the Upper Room, 1921
SCHWEITZER, A., Quest of the Historical Jesus, 1910

BARTLET and CARLYLE, Christianity in History, 1917
GORE, C., Holy Spirit and the Church, 1924
KIRSOPP LAKE, Body of Christ, 1901 ; Earlier Epistles of S. Paul, 1911
KNOX, W., S. Paul and the Church of Jerusalem, 1925
SCHWEITZER, A., Paul and his Interpreters, 1912

Mediaeval and Modern Periods—
BETHUNE-BAKER, Early History of Christian Doctrine, 1903
COULTON, G. G., Five Centuries of Religion, 1923
HARNACK, A., History of Dogma, 1896 ; Mission and Expansion of Christianity, 1904
STONE, D., Doctrine of the Holy Eucharist, 1909

SELECTED BOOK LIST

Cambridge Modern History (vol. ii.), 1903
GIBSON, E. C. S., The Thirty-Nine Articles, 1906
PROCTER and FRERE, New History of the Book of Common Prayer, 1905
PULLAN, L., Religion since the Reformation, 1923
WEBB, C. C. J., Religious Thought in the Oxford Movement, 1928
WACE and BUCHEIM, Luther's Primary Works, 1883

ILLINGWORTH, J. R., Divine Transcendence, 1911
QUICK, O., Christian Sacraments, 1927
STRONG, T. B., Doctrine of the Real Presence, 1899

HÜGEL, F. VON, Mystical Element in Religion, 1909
INGE, W. R., Christian Mysticism, 1899
UNDERHILL, E., Mysticism, 1911

Confirmation (S.P.C.K.), 1926
LACEY, T. A., Marriage in Church and State, 1912
PULLER, F. W., Anointing of the Sick, 1904
STONE, D., Holy Baptism, 1899
WATKINS, O. D., History of Penance, 1917
WHITHAM, A. R., Holy Orders, 1910

INDEX

ABRAHAMS, 96 n., 98.
Agape, the, and the Eucharist, 112 f.
'Am-Ha'arez, the, 75
Animism, 13, 16
Apocalypses, the, 75
Apuleius, 63.
Aquinas, S. Thomas, 128, 132, 137
ASTLEY, 12
Athanasius, S., 121
Augustine, S., 126 f., 132

Baptism, Egyptian, 6
— Jesus and, 89 f.
— in the Apostolic Church, 95 f.
— 'in the name of Jesus,' 97
BARTLET, V., 56 n.
BARTLET and CARLYLE, 103 n., 114 n.
Berengar of Tours, 135, 143
Bernard, S., 132
BERTHOLET, 69, 81
BEZZANT, 96 n.
BILLOT, 130
BLACKMAN, 6 n.
Black Rubric, the, 148
Bonaventure, S., 128
BOULANGER, 75
BOUSSET, 68, 92
BROWNING, 139
Burnt offering, 34 f.

Calvin, 144 f.
Ceremonies, primitive, 5 f.
— Hebrew, 20 f.

Christianity and the Mystery Cults, 67
Church of England and Sacramental theory, 145 f.
Clement of Alexandria, 62, 117
Communicatio Idiomatum, 89
Consubstantiation, 143
COULTON, 139
Covenant, ratification of, 39
Cultus, the, 20
— attitude of the prophets towards, 47 f.
Cybele, cult of, 62
Cyprian, S., 120
Cyril of Jerusalem, S., 125

Damien, S. Peter, 133
Deuteronomic Law, the, 17
— — Jeremiah's attitude towards, 48 f.
Dionysius of Alexandria, 117
Dionysus, cult of, 59.
Donne, 146
DRIVER, 24

Eleusinian mysteries, the, 61
Elizabeth, Queen, 41
Essenes, the, 76
Eucharist, the, suggested origin of, 79
— Supper of the Lord and, 88 f., 102 f.
— the Ante-Nicene Fathers and, 114 f.

172 SACRAMENTALISM

Eucharist, medieval theology and, 134 f.
— the Church of England and, 147 f., 156 f.
— the Eastern Church and, 150

FAIRWEATHER, 68, 71 n.
FRAZER, 12

Galilee, Gentile influence in, 72 f.
GAVIN, 90 n.
GAYFORD, 32, 37 n., 41
GLOVER, 82
Gnosticism, 60
GOUDGE, 34, 43 n., 88 n.
GRAY, 31, 37 n., 39 n., 41, 68, 72 n.
Gregory of Nyssa, 125
GRENFELL and HUNT, 66 n.

HALLIDAY, 63 n.
HARNACK, 113, 117
HASTINGS, 73 n.
HEADLAM, 72 n., 74
Hellenism, 71
Hooker, 147
HOSKYNS, 107
Hugh of S. Victor, 132

Idolatry, 51, 53 f.
Ignatius, S., 115
Initiation, 5 f., 25, 61, 95
Irenæus, S., 115
Isis, cult of, 63

JACOBS, 142 n.
JAMES, 9
JEVONS, 57
John of Damascus, 126
Josephus, 27 n.
Justin Martyr, 2, 64, 115

KENNEDY, 64 n.
Kiddush, the, 78

LACEY, 130 n.

LAKE, 94
Lanfranc, 136
Lateran, Fourth Council of the, 136
LIETZMANN, 105
LOEWE, 73
Lombard, Peter, 136
LOWIE, 14 n.
Luther, 141 f.
Lyons, Council of, 137

MACCHIORO, 74
Magic and religion, 12 f.
' Mana,' 4
Marburg Conference, Luther at the, 143
MARETT, 14 n.
Materialism, 51
Mithras, cult of, 64
MOORE, 90 n.
MURRAY, 65

NAIRNE, 4
Nature, sacramental view of, 3 f.
— Hebrew view of, 18 f.
— Greek view of, 58
NEWMAN, 150

OESTERLEY, 76, 81 n.
OESTERLEY and BOX, 68 n., 78 n.
Origen, 117
Orpheus, cult of, 59
OTTO, R., 3
Otto of Bamberg, 132

Passover, the, 38
— and the Last Supper, 78 f., 85 f.
Peace offering, 33, 51
PEAKE, 55 n.
PLUMMER, 91
PRESCOTT, 1
PULLAN, 151

QUICK, 85 n., 158

INDEX 173

Radbert, Paschasius, 135
Ratramn, 135
Receptionism, 145
REHM, 13
RELTON, 139 n.
ROBINSON, 41 n., 54
ROPES, 81 n.
ROSSETTI, 36

Sacrament, the word, vii, 7, 131
— the, and the virtue of the sacrament, 127
Sacraments, the, and scholastic theology, 128 f.
— and the XXXIX Articles, 147 f.
— number of, 131 f.
Sacramental principle, the, 2
Sacramental modes, 4 f.
— persons, 21
Sacrifice, primitive, 9
— meaning of, in O.T., 31 f.
— attitude of the prophets towards, 44 f.
SANDAY, 24 n., 75
Savoy Conference, 147
SCHLATTER, 110 n.
SCHULTZ, 25, 42
SCHWEITZER, 79, 82
Shema, 29

SIMPSON, 48 n.
Sin offering, 36
SKINNER, 48, 50
SMITH, ROBERTSON, 9, 26, 31, 52
SPENS, 157
STONE, 42, 116, 139 n., 150 n., 151 n., 152
STREETER, 69
Suarez, 130
Supper of the Lord, the, 85 f.
— and the Eucharist, 88 f.
— in the Apostolic Church, 102 f.

Taboo, 6, 8
TACHAU, 73
TEMPLE, 156
Tertullian, 2, 118, 121
Totemistic systems, 8
Transubstantiation, 136, 139, 150
Trent, Council of, 129, 132, 137, 147, 149
Trespass offering, 36
TRUC, 14 n., 110

VÖLKER, 113

WILLIAMS, N. P., 79, 95, 99 n., 103

For Product Safety Concerns and Information please contact our EU
representative GPSR@taylorandfrancis.com
Taylor & Francis Verlag GmbH, Kaufingerstraße 24, 80331 München, Germany

www.ingramcontent.com/pod-product-compliance
Lightning Source LLC
Chambersburg PA
CBHW061448300426
44114CB00014B/1891